D0515697

PIKES PEAK LIBRARY DISTRICT

NO LONGER
PROPERTY OF PPLD

16608874 0

THE FACTS
IN THE CASE OF
THE DEPARTURE OF
❧ MISS FINCH ❧

Story by
NEIL GAIMAN

Art by
MICHAEL ZULLI

Lettering and
script adaptation by
TODD KLEIN

With special thanks to
OLGA NUNES

DARK HORSE BOOKS®

Editor
Diana Schutz

Assistant Editors
Dave Marshall & Katie Moody

Book Design
Tony Ong

Digital Production
Chris Horn

Publisher
Mike Richardson

The Facts in the Case of the Departure of Miss Finch™ © 2008 Neil Gaiman. All rights reserved. Artwork © 2008 Michael Zulli. All rights reserved. All other material, unless otherwise specified, © 2008 Dark Horse Comics, Inc. Miss Finch and the likeness of all characters featured herein are trademarks of Neil Gaiman. Dark Horse Books® and the Dark Horse logo are registered trademarks of Dark Horse Comics, Inc. No portion of this publication may be reproduced or transmitted, in any form or by any means, without the express written permission of the copyright holders. Names, characters, places, and incidents featured in this publication either are the product of the author's imagination or are used fictitiously. Any resemblance to actual persons (living or dead), events, institutions, or locales, without satiric intent, is coincidental.

Published by Dark Horse Books
A division of Dark Horse Comics, Inc.
10956 SE Main Street
Milwaukie, Oregon 97222
United States of America

darkhorse.com

First Edition: January 2008
ISBN 978-1-59307-667-2

1 3 5 7 9 10 8 6 4 2

PRINTED IN CHINA

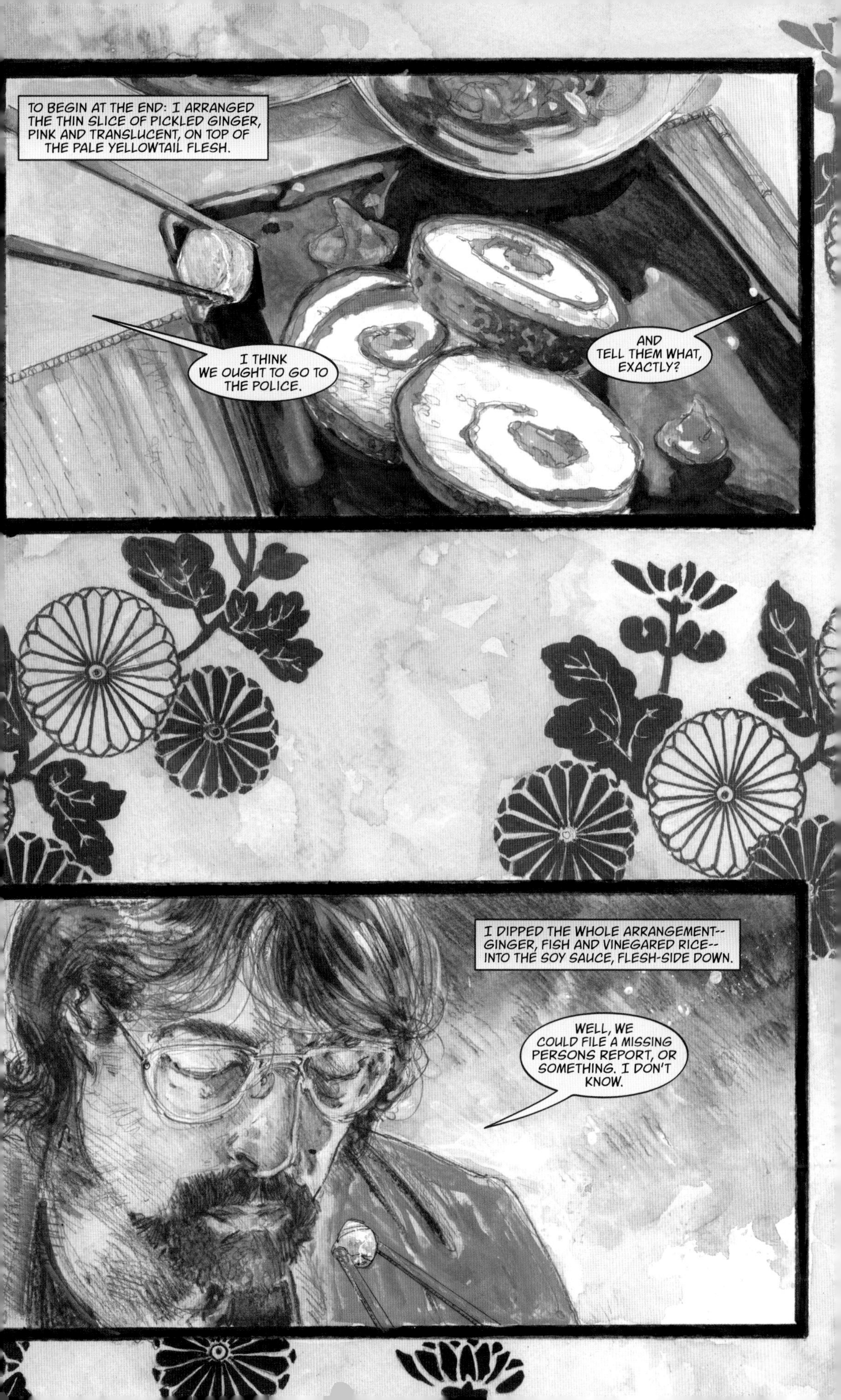
TO BEGIN AT THE END: I ARRANGED THE THIN SLICE OF PICKLED GINGER, PINK AND TRANSLUCENT, ON TOP OF THE PALE YELLOWTAIL FLESH.
I THINK WE OUGHT TO GO TO THE POLICE.
AND TELL THEM WHAT, EXACTLY?
I DIPPED THE WHOLE ARRANGEMENT--GINGER, FISH AND VINEGARED RICE--INTO THE SOY SAUCE, FLESH-SIDE DOWN.
WELL, WE COULD FILE A MISSING PERSONS REPORT, OR SOMETHING. I DON'T KNOW.

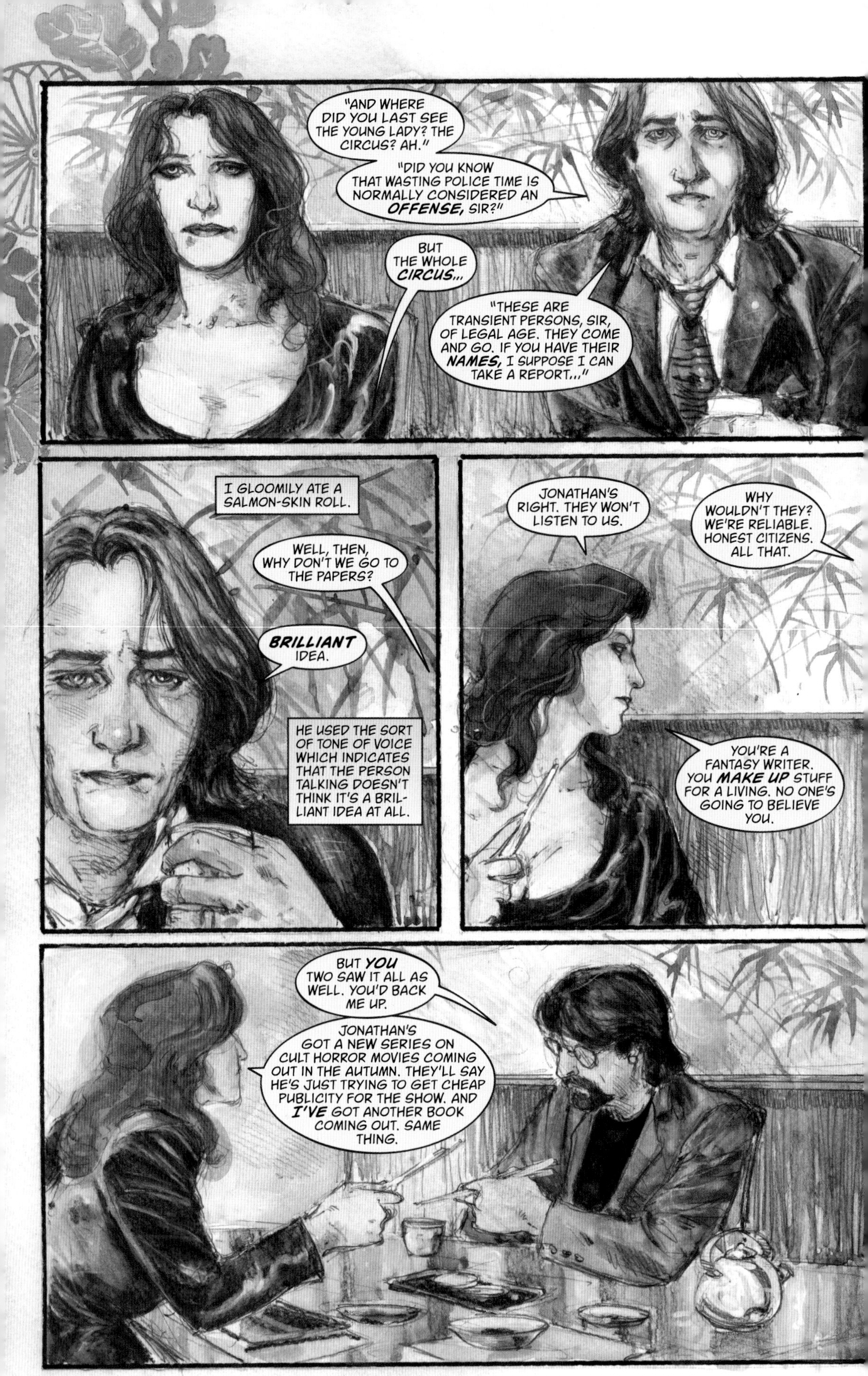

"AND WHERE DID YOU LAST SEE THE YOUNG LADY? THE CIRCUS? AH."
"DID YOU KNOW THAT WASTING POLICE TIME IS NORMALLY CONSIDERED AN OFFENSE, SIR?"
BUT THE WHOLE CIRCUS...
"THESE ARE TRANSIENT PERSONS, SIR, OF LEGAL AGE. THEY COME AND GO. IF YOU HAVE THEIR NAMES, I SUPPOSE I CAN TAKE A REPORT..."
I GLOOMILY ATE A SALMON-SKIN ROLL.
WELL, THEN, WHY DON'T WE GO TO THE PAPERS?
BRILLIANT IDEA.
HE USED THE SORT OF TONE OF VOICE WHICH INDICATES THAT THE PERSON TALKING DOESN'T THINK IT'S A BRIL-LIANT IDEA AT ALL.
JONATHAN'S RIGHT. THEY WON'T LISTEN TO US.
WHY WOULDN'T THEY? WE'RE RELIABLE. HONEST CITIZENS. ALL THAT.
YOU'RE A FANTASY WRITER. YOU MAKE UP STUFF FOR A LIVING. NO ONE'S GOING TO BELIEVE YOU.
BUT YOU TWO SAW IT ALL AS WELL. YOU'D BACK ME UP.
JONATHAN'S GOT A NEW SERIES ON CULT HORROR MOVIES COMING OUT IN THE AUTUMN. THEY'LL SAY HE'S JUST TRYING TO GET CHEAP PUBLICITY FOR THE SHOW. AND I'VE GOT ANOTHER BOOK COMING OUT. SAME THING.

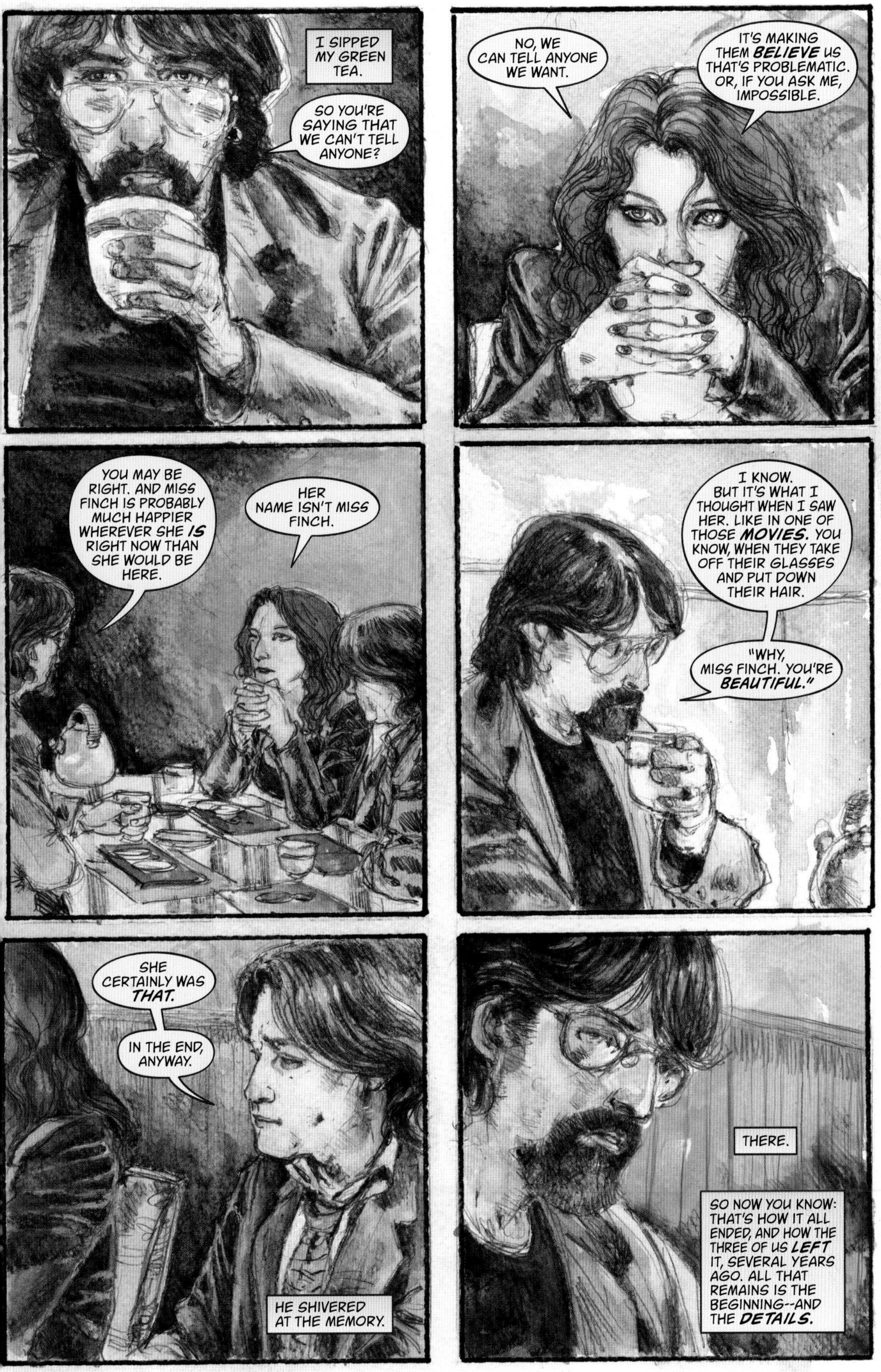
I SIPPED MY GREEN TEA.
SO YOU'RE SAYING THAT WE CAN'T TELL ANYONE?
NO, WE CAN TELL ANYONE WE WANT.
IT'S MAKING THEM BELIEVE US THAT'S PROBLEMATIC. OR, IF YOU ASK ME, IMPOSSIBLE.
YOU MAY BE RIGHT. AND MISS FINCH IS PROBABLY MUCH HAPPIER WHEREVER SHE IS RIGHT NOW THAN SHE WOULD BE HERE.
HER NAME ISN'T MISS FINCH.
I KNOW. BUT IT'S WHAT I THOUGHT WHEN I SAW HER. LIKE IN ONE OF THOSE MOVIES. YOU KNOW, WHEN THEY TAKE OFF THEIR GLASSES AND PUT DOWN THEIR HAIR.
"WHY, MISS FINCH. YOU'RE BEAUTIFUL."
SHE CERTAINLY WAS THAT.
IN THE END, ANYWAY.
HE SHIVERED AT THE MEMORY.
THERE.
SO NOW YOU KNOW: THAT'S HOW IT ALL ENDED, AND HOW THE THREE OF US LEFT IT, SEVERAL YEARS AGO. ALL THAT REMAINS IS THE BEGINNING--AND THE DETAILS.

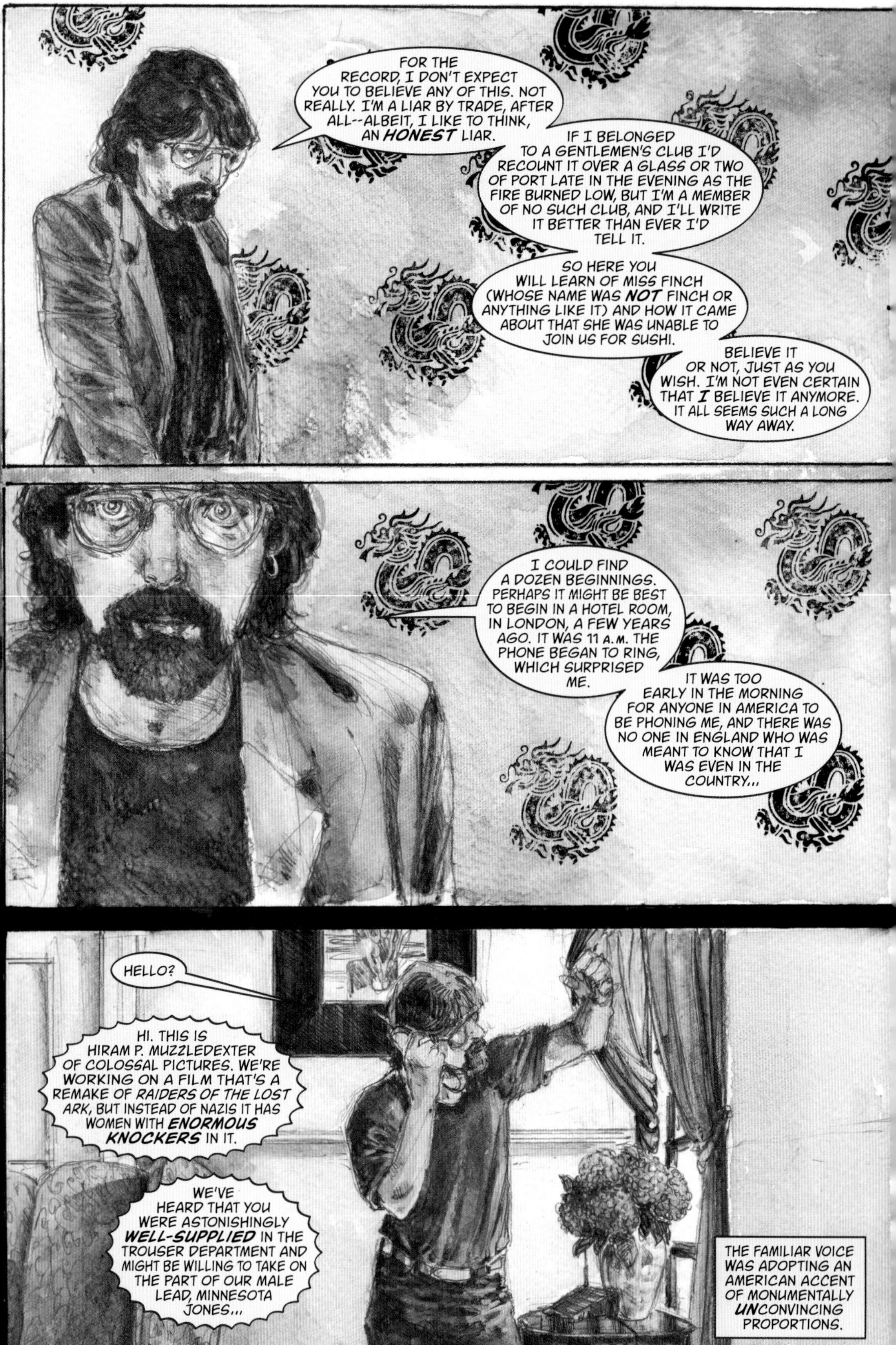
FOR THE RECORD, I DON'T EXPECT YOU TO BELIEVE ANY OF THIS. NOT REALLY. I'M A LIAR BY TRADE, AFTER ALL--ALBEIT, I LIKE TO THINK, AN **HONEST** LIAR.
IF I BELONGED TO A GENTLEMEN'S CLUB I'D RECOUNT IT OVER A GLASS OR TWO OF PORT LATE IN THE EVENING AS THE FIRE BURNED LOW, BUT I'M A MEMBER OF NO SUCH CLUB, AND I'LL WRITE IT BETTER THAN EVER I'D TELL IT.
SO HERE YOU WILL LEARN OF MISS FINCH (WHOSE NAME WAS **NOT** FINCH OR ANYTHING LIKE IT) AND HOW IT CAME ABOUT THAT SHE WAS UNABLE TO JOIN US FOR SUSHI.
BELIEVE IT OR NOT, JUST AS YOU WISH. I'M NOT EVEN CERTAIN THAT ***I*** BELIEVE IT ANYMORE. IT ALL SEEMS SUCH A LONG WAY AWAY.
I COULD FIND A DOZEN BEGINNINGS. PERHAPS IT MIGHT BE BEST TO BEGIN IN A HOTEL ROOM, IN LONDON, A FEW YEARS AGO. IT WAS 11 A.M. THE PHONE BEGAN TO RING, WHICH SURPRISED ME.
IT WAS TOO EARLY IN THE MORNING FOR ANYONE IN AMERICA TO BE PHONING ME, AND THERE WAS NO ONE IN ENGLAND WHO WAS MEANT TO KNOW THAT I WAS EVEN IN THE COUNTRY...
HELLO?
HI. THIS IS HIRAM P. MUZZLEDEXTER OF COLOSSAL PICTURES. WE'RE WORKING ON A FILM THAT'S A REMAKE OF *RAIDERS OF THE LOST ARK*, BUT INSTEAD OF NAZIS IT HAS WOMEN WITH ***ENORMOUS KNOCKERS*** IN IT.
WE'VE HEARD THAT YOU WERE ASTONISHINGLY ***WELL-SUPPLIED*** IN THE TROUSER DEPARTMENT AND MIGHT BE WILLING TO TAKE ON THE PART OF OUR MALE LEAD, MINNESOTA JONES...
THE FAMILIAR VOICE WAS ADOPTING AN AMERICAN ACCENT OF MONUMENTALLY ***UN***CONVINCING PROPORTIONS.

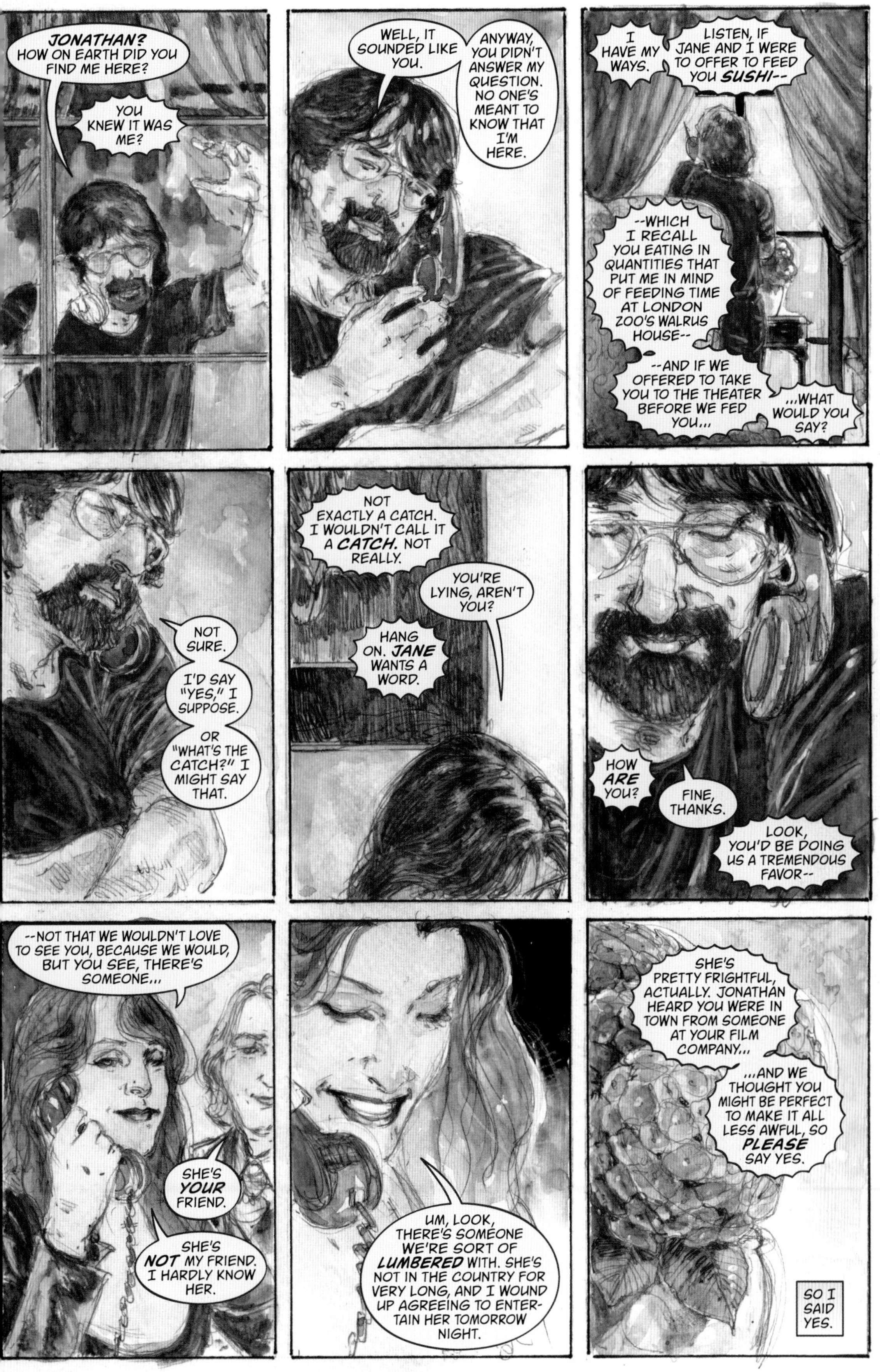

JONATHAN? HOW ON EARTH DID YOU FIND ME HERE?
YOU KNEW IT WAS ME?
WELL, IT SOUNDED LIKE YOU.
ANYWAY, YOU DIDN'T ANSWER MY QUESTION. NO ONE'S MEANT TO KNOW THAT I'M HERE.
I HAVE MY WAYS.
LISTEN, IF JANE AND I WERE TO OFFER TO FEED YOU SUSHI--
--WHICH I RECALL YOU EATING IN QUANTITIES THAT PUT ME IN MIND OF FEEDING TIME AT LONDON ZOO'S WALRUS HOUSE--
--AND IF WE OFFERED TO TAKE YOU TO THE THEATER BEFORE WE FED YOU...
...WHAT WOULD YOU SAY?
NOT SURE.
I'D SAY "YES," I SUPPOSE.
OR "WHAT'S THE CATCH?" I MIGHT SAY THAT.
NOT EXACTLY A CATCH. I WOULDN'T CALL IT A CATCH. NOT REALLY.
YOU'RE LYING, AREN'T YOU?
HANG ON. JANE WANTS A WORD.
HOW ARE YOU?
FINE, THANKS.
LOOK, YOU'D BE DOING US A TREMENDOUS FAVOR--
--NOT THAT WE WOULDN'T LOVE TO SEE YOU, BECAUSE WE WOULD, BUT YOU SEE, THERE'S SOMEONE...
SHE'S YOUR FRIEND.
SHE'S NOT MY FRIEND. I HARDLY KNOW HER.
UM, LOOK, THERE'S SOMEONE WE'RE SORT OF LUMBERED WITH. SHE'S NOT IN THE COUNTRY FOR VERY LONG, AND I WOUND UP AGREEING TO ENTERTAIN HER TOMORROW NIGHT.
SHE'S PRETTY FRIGHTFUL, ACTUALLY. JONATHAN HEARD YOU WERE IN TOWN FROM SOMEONE AT YOUR FILM COMPANY...
...AND WE THOUGHT YOU MIGHT BE PERFECT TO MAKE IT ALL LESS AWFUL, SO PLEASE SAY YES.
SO I SAID YES.

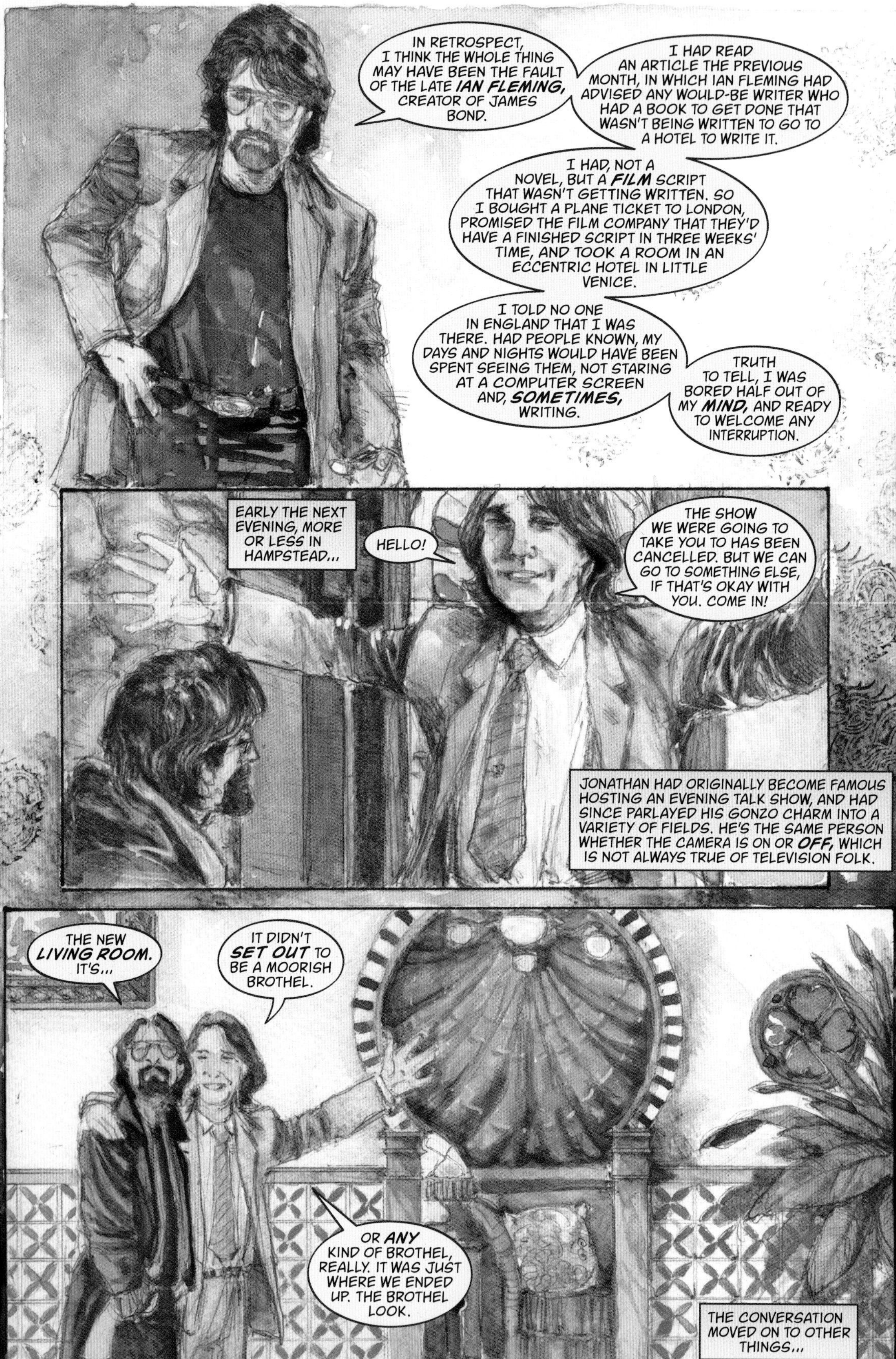
IN RETROSPECT, I THINK THE WHOLE THING MAY HAVE BEEN THE FAULT OF THE LATE IAN FLEMING, CREATOR OF JAMES BOND.
I HAD READ AN ARTICLE THE PREVIOUS MONTH, IN WHICH IAN FLEMING HAD ADVISED ANY WOULD-BE WRITER WHO HAD A BOOK TO GET DONE THAT WASN'T BEING WRITTEN TO GO TO A HOTEL TO WRITE IT.
I HAD, NOT A NOVEL, BUT A FILM SCRIPT THAT WASN'T GETTING WRITTEN. SO I BOUGHT A PLANE TICKET TO LONDON, PROMISED THE FILM COMPANY THAT THEY'D HAVE A FINISHED SCRIPT IN THREE WEEKS' TIME, AND TOOK A ROOM IN AN ECCENTRIC HOTEL IN LITTLE VENICE.
I TOLD NO ONE IN ENGLAND THAT I WAS THERE. HAD PEOPLE KNOWN, MY DAYS AND NIGHTS WOULD HAVE BEEN SPENT SEEING THEM, NOT STARING AT A COMPUTER SCREEN AND, SOMETIMES, WRITING.
TRUTH TO TELL, I WAS BORED HALF OUT OF MY MIND, AND READY TO WELCOME ANY INTERRUPTION.
EARLY THE NEXT EVENING, MORE OR LESS IN HAMPSTEAD...
HELLO!
THE SHOW WE WERE GOING TO TAKE YOU TO HAS BEEN CANCELLED. BUT WE CAN GO TO SOMETHING ELSE, IF THAT'S OKAY WITH YOU. COME IN!
JONATHAN HAD ORIGINALLY BECOME FAMOUS HOSTING AN EVENING TALK SHOW, AND HAD SINCE PARLAYED HIS GONZO CHARM INTO A VARIETY OF FIELDS. HE'S THE SAME PERSON WHETHER THE CAMERA IS ON OR OFF, WHICH IS NOT ALWAYS TRUE OF TELEVISION FOLK.
THE NEW LIVING ROOM. IT'S...
IT DIDN'T SET OUT TO BE A MOORISH BROTHEL.
OR ANY KIND OF BROTHEL, REALLY. IT WAS JUST WHERE WE ENDED UP. THE BROTHEL LOOK.
THE CONVERSATION MOVED ON TO OTHER THINGS...

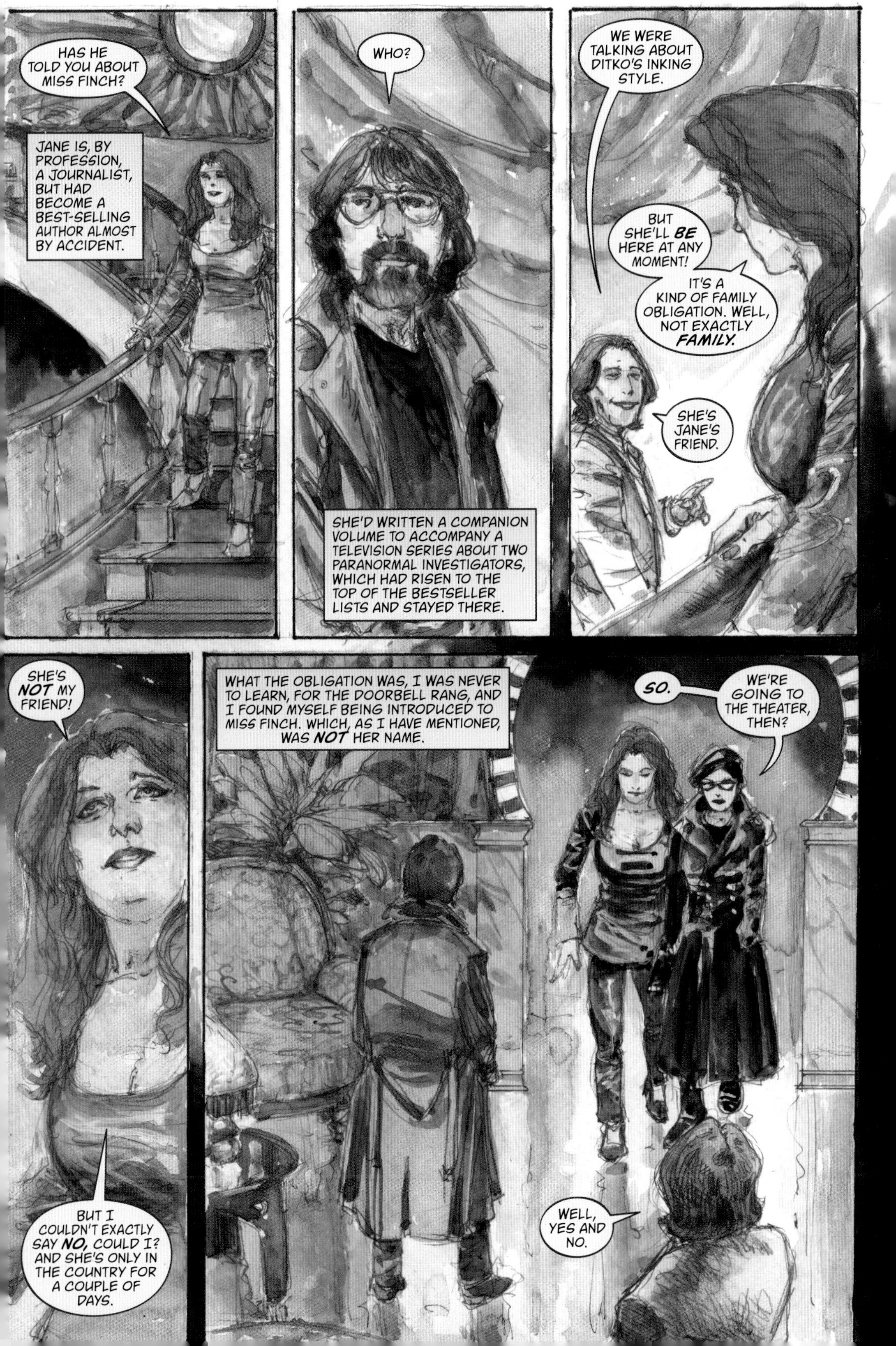
HAS HE TOLD YOU ABOUT MISS FINCH?
JANE IS, BY PROFESSION, A JOURNALIST, BUT HAD BECOME A BEST-SELLING AUTHOR ALMOST BY ACCIDENT.
WHO?
SHE'D WRITTEN A COMPANION VOLUME TO ACCOMPANY A TELEVISION SERIES ABOUT TWO PARANORMAL INVESTIGATORS, WHICH HAD RISEN TO THE TOP OF THE BESTSELLER LISTS AND STAYED THERE.
WE WERE TALKING ABOUT DITKO'S INKING STYLE.
BUT SHE'LL **BE** HERE AT ANY MOMENT!
IT'S A KIND OF FAMILY OBLIGATION. WELL, NOT EXACTLY **FAMILY.**
SHE'S JANE'S FRIEND.
SHE'S **NOT** MY FRIEND!
BUT I COULDN'T EXACTLY SAY **NO,** COULD I? AND SHE'S ONLY IN THE COUNTRY FOR A COUPLE OF DAYS.
WHAT THE OBLIGATION WAS, I WAS NEVER TO LEARN, FOR THE DOORBELL RANG, AND I FOUND MYSELF BEING INTRODUCED TO MISS FINCH. WHICH, AS I HAVE MENTIONED, WAS **NOT** HER NAME.
SO.
WE'RE GOING TO THE THEATER, THEN?
WELL, YES AND NO.

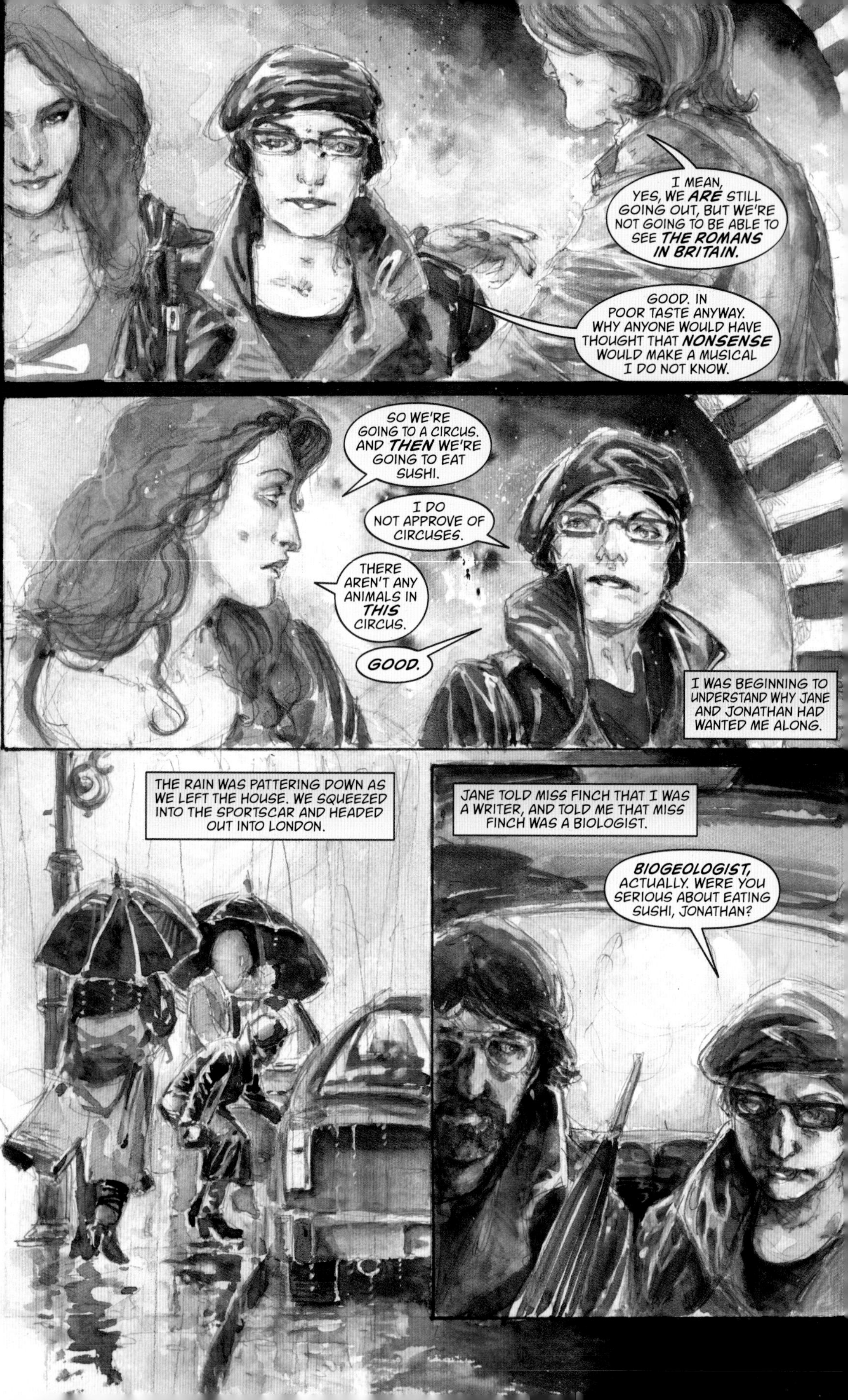
I MEAN, YES, WE ARE STILL GOING OUT, BUT WE'RE NOT GOING TO BE ABLE TO SEE THE ROMANS IN BRITAIN.
GOOD. IN POOR TASTE ANYWAY. WHY ANYONE WOULD HAVE THOUGHT THAT NONSENSE WOULD MAKE A MUSICAL I DO NOT KNOW.
SO WE'RE GOING TO A CIRCUS. AND THEN WE'RE GOING TO EAT SUSHI.
I DO NOT APPROVE OF CIRCUSES.
THERE AREN'T ANY ANIMALS IN THIS CIRCUS.
GOOD.
I WAS BEGINNING TO UNDERSTAND WHY JANE AND JONATHAN HAD WANTED ME ALONG.
THE RAIN WAS PATTERING DOWN AS WE LEFT THE HOUSE. WE SQUEEZED INTO THE SPORTSCAR AND HEADED OUT INTO LONDON.
JANE TOLD MISS FINCH THAT I WAS A WRITER, AND TOLD ME THAT MISS FINCH WAS A BIOLOGIST.
BIOGEOLOGIST, ACTUALLY. WERE YOU SERIOUS ABOUT EATING SUSHI, JONATHAN?

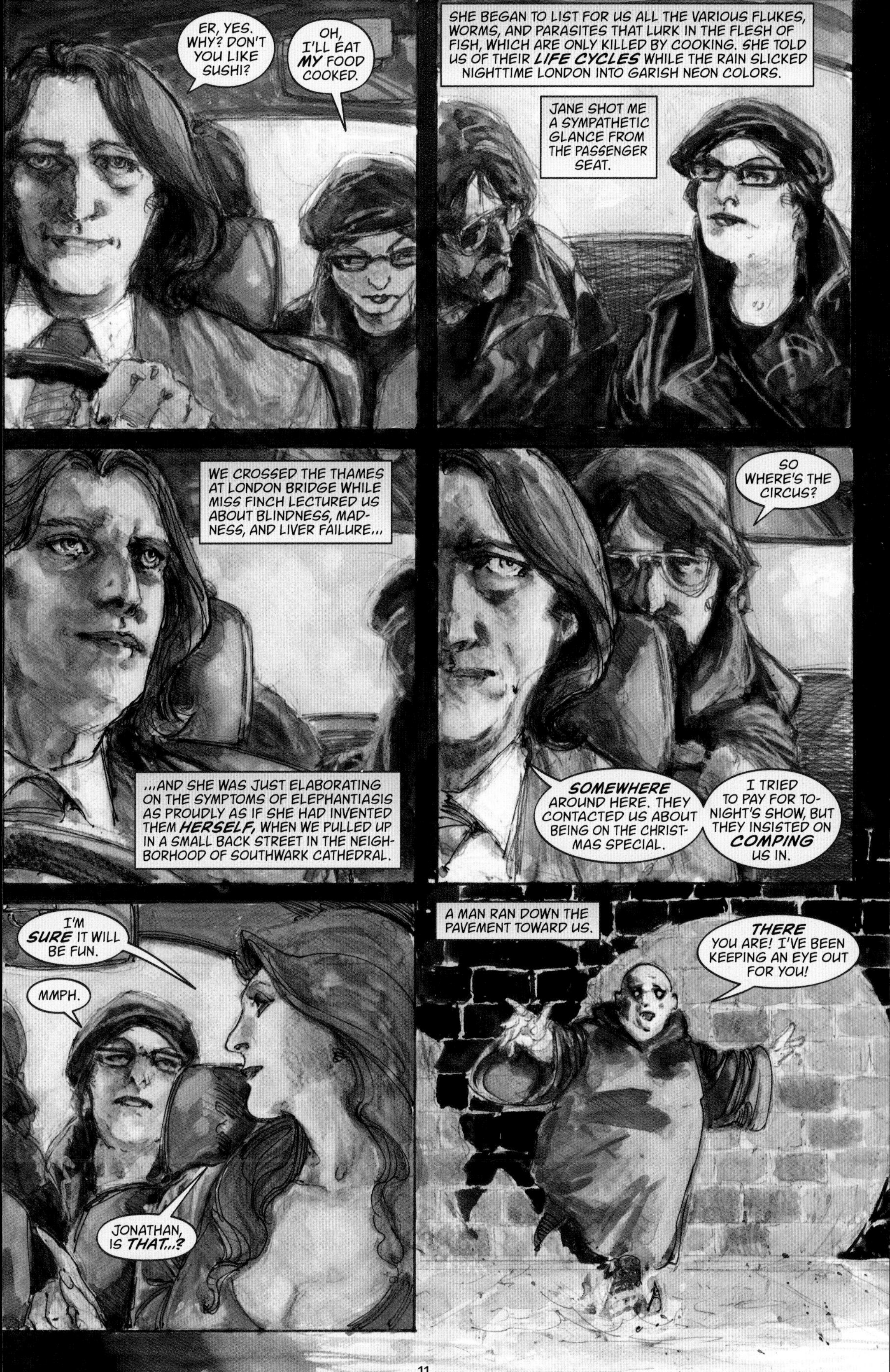

ER, YES. WHY? DON'T YOU LIKE SUSHI?
OH, I'LL EAT MY FOOD COOKED.
SHE BEGAN TO LIST FOR US ALL THE VARIOUS FLUKES, WORMS, AND PARASITES THAT LURK IN THE FLESH OF FISH, WHICH ARE ONLY KILLED BY COOKING. SHE TOLD US OF THEIR LIFE CYCLES WHILE THE RAIN SLICKED NIGHTTIME LONDON INTO GARISH NEON COLORS.
JANE SHOT ME A SYMPATHETIC GLANCE FROM THE PASSENGER SEAT.
WE CROSSED THE THAMES AT LONDON BRIDGE WHILE MISS FINCH LECTURED US ABOUT BLINDNESS, MADNESS, AND LIVER FAILURE...
...AND SHE WAS JUST ELABORATING ON THE SYMPTOMS OF ELEPHANTIASIS AS PROUDLY AS IF SHE HAD INVENTED THEM HERSELF, WHEN WE PULLED UP IN A SMALL BACK STREET IN THE NEIGHBORHOOD OF SOUTHWARK CATHEDRAL.
SO WHERE'S THE CIRCUS?
SOMEWHERE AROUND HERE. THEY CONTACTED US ABOUT BEING ON THE CHRISTMAS SPECIAL.
I TRIED TO PAY FOR TONIGHT'S SHOW, BUT THEY INSISTED ON COMPING US IN.
I'M SURE IT WILL BE FUN.
MMPH.
JONATHAN, IS THAT...?
A MAN RAN DOWN THE PAVEMENT TOWARD US.
THERE YOU ARE! I'VE BEEN KEEPING AN EYE OUT FOR YOU!

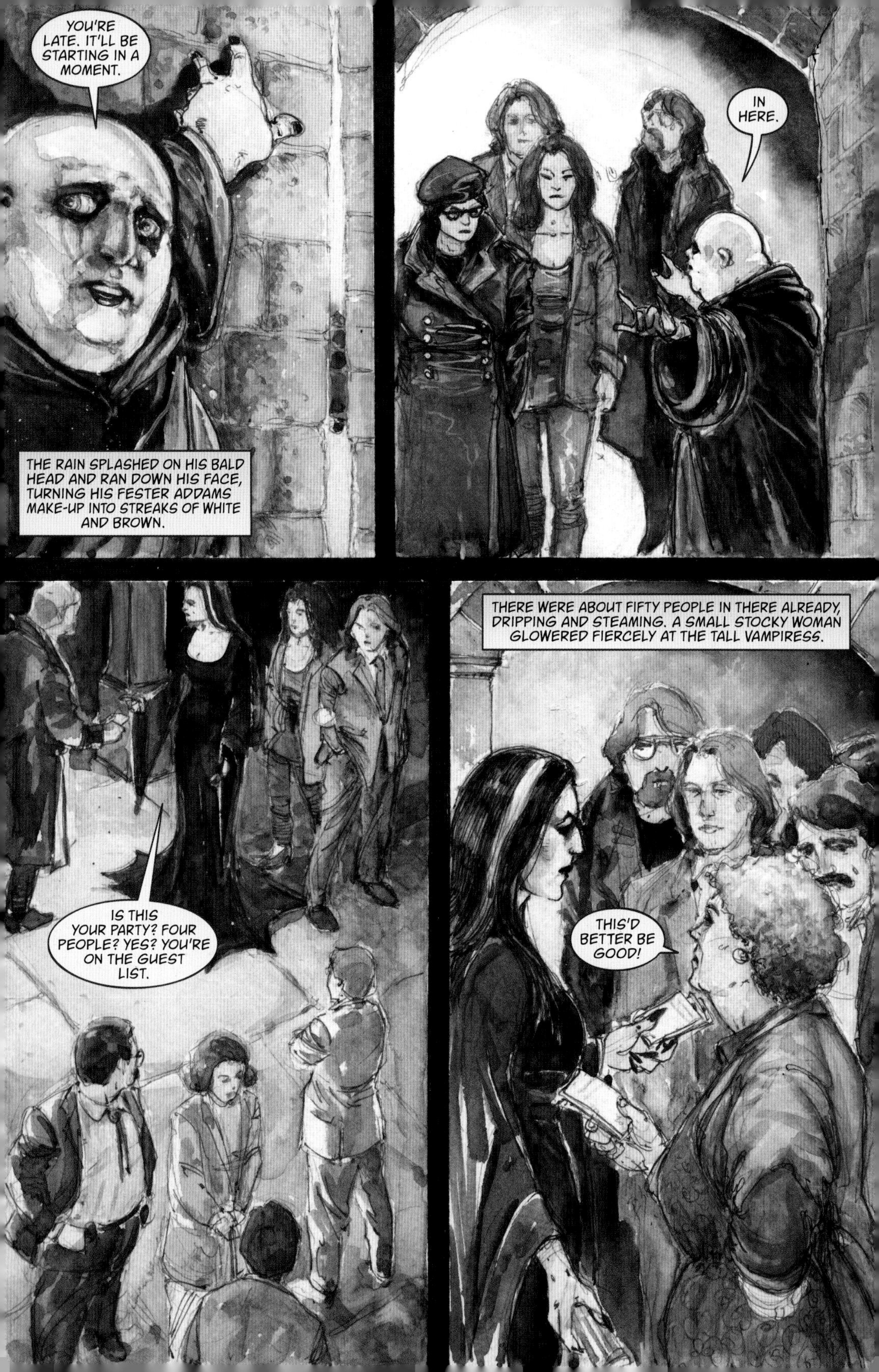

YOU'RE LATE. IT'LL BE STARTING IN A MOMENT.
THE RAIN SPLASHED ON HIS BALD HEAD AND RAN DOWN HIS FACE, TURNING HIS FESTER ADDAMS MAKE-UP INTO STREAKS OF WHITE AND BROWN.
IN HERE.
IS THIS YOUR PARTY? FOUR PEOPLE? YES? YOU'RE ON THE GUEST LIST.
THERE WERE ABOUT FIFTY PEOPLE IN THERE ALREADY, DRIPPING AND STEAMING. A SMALL STOCKY WOMAN GLOWERED FIERCELY AT THE TALL VAMPIRESS.
THIS'D BETTER BE GOOD!

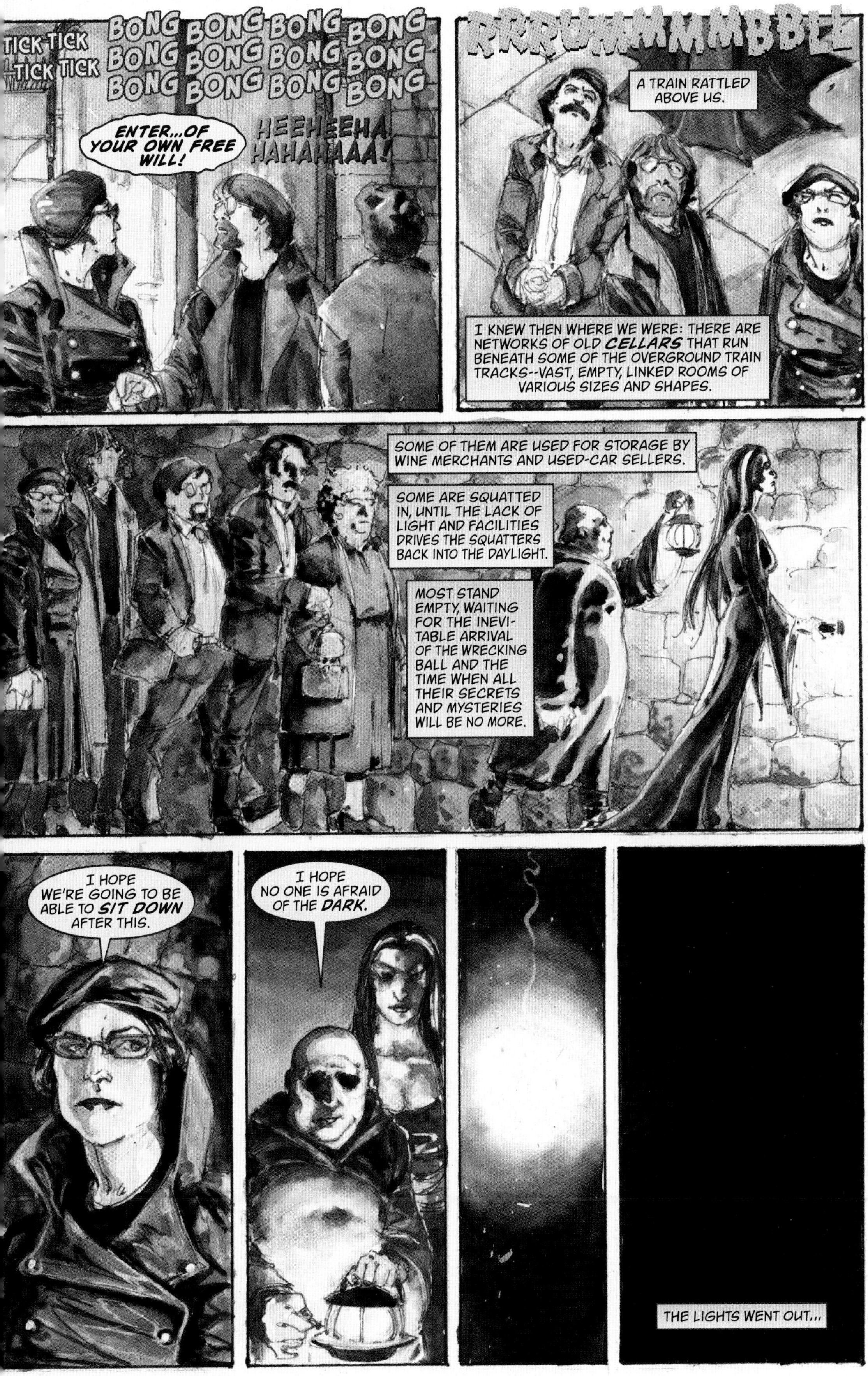
TICK TICK
TICK TICK
BONG BONG BONG BONG
BONG BONG BONG BONG
BONG BONG BONG BONG
ENTER...OF YOUR OWN FREE WILL!
HEEHEEHA HAHAHAAA!
RRRUMMMMBBLE
A TRAIN RATTLED ABOVE US.
I KNEW THEN WHERE WE WERE: THERE ARE NETWORKS OF OLD CELLARS THAT RUN BENEATH SOME OF THE OVERGROUND TRAIN TRACKS--VAST, EMPTY, LINKED ROOMS OF VARIOUS SIZES AND SHAPES.
SOME OF THEM ARE USED FOR STORAGE BY WINE MERCHANTS AND USED-CAR SELLERS.
SOME ARE SQUATTED IN, UNTIL THE LACK OF LIGHT AND FACILITIES DRIVES THE SQUATTERS BACK INTO THE DAYLIGHT.
MOST STAND EMPTY, WAITING FOR THE INEVITABLE ARRIVAL OF THE WRECKING BALL AND THE TIME WHEN ALL THEIR SECRETS AND MYSTERIES WILL BE NO MORE.
I HOPE WE'RE GOING TO BE ABLE TO SIT DOWN AFTER THIS.
I HOPE NO ONE IS AFRAID OF THE DARK.
THE LIGHTS WENT OUT...

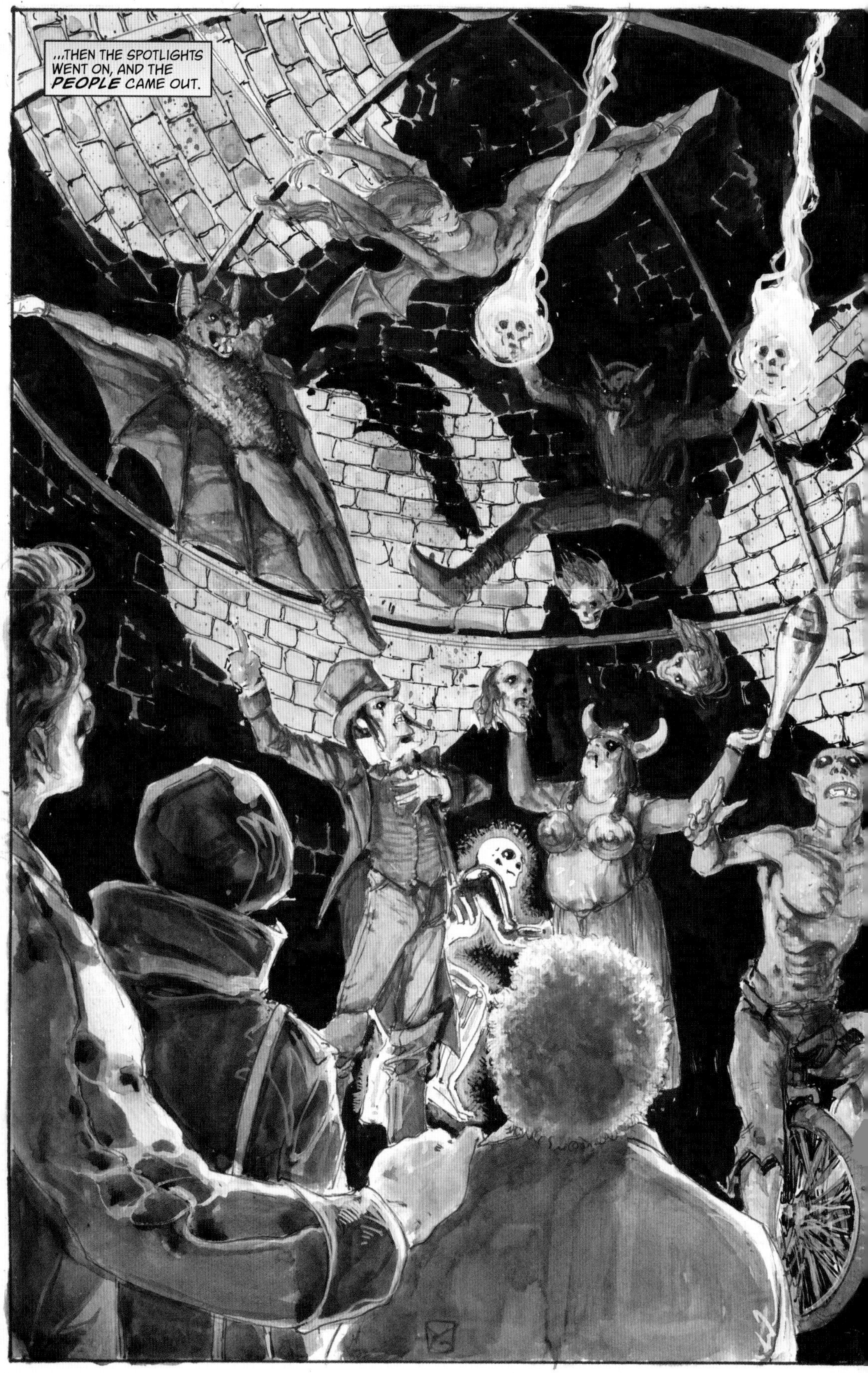
...THEN THE SPOTLIGHTS WENT ON, AND THE PEOPLE CAME OUT.

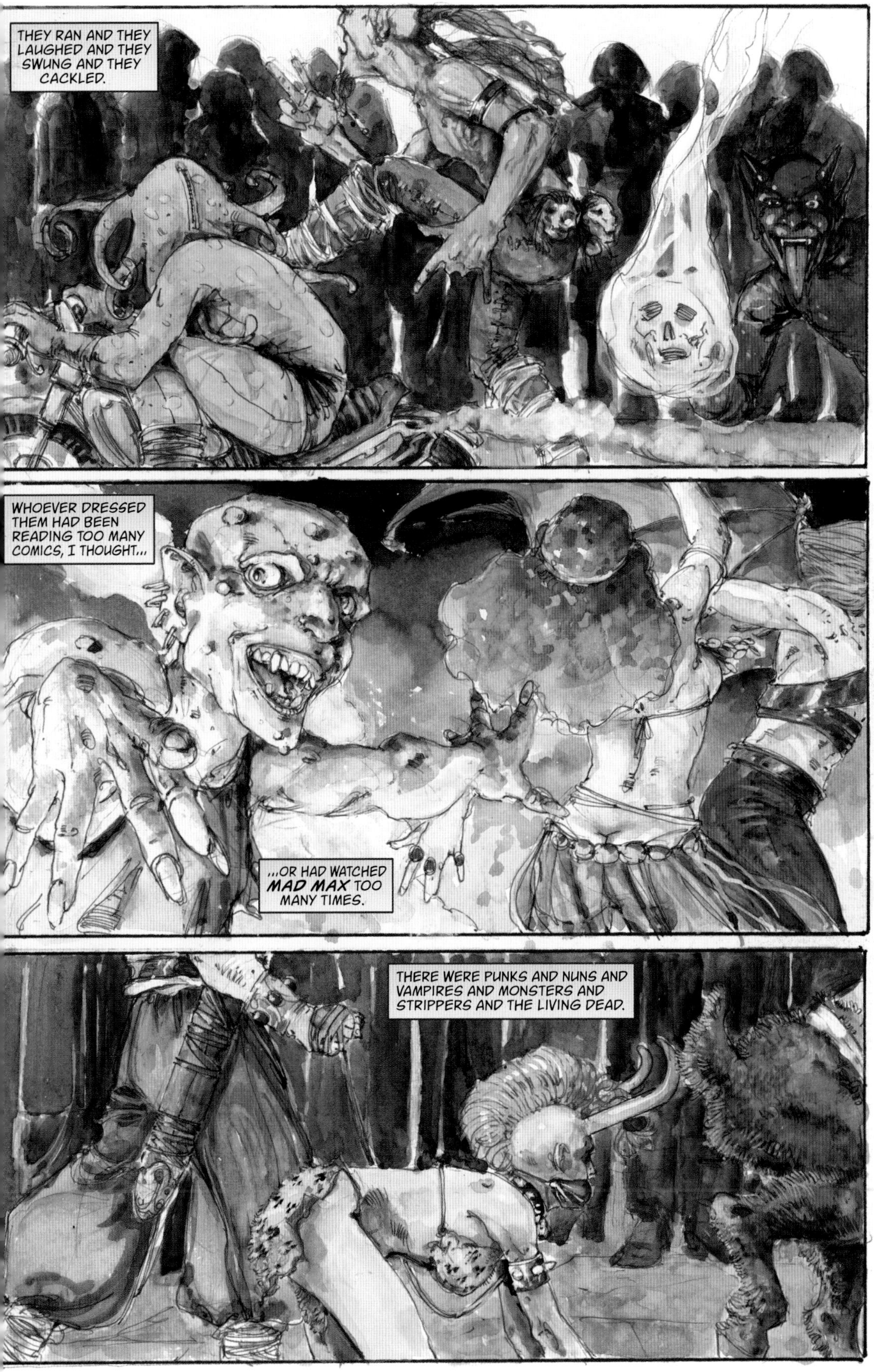
THEY RAN AND THEY LAUGHED AND THEY SWUNG AND THEY CACKLED.
WHOEVER DRESSED THEM HAD BEEN READING TOO MANY COMICS, I THOUGHT...
...OR HAD WATCHED ***MAD MAX*** TOO MANY TIMES.
THERE WERE PUNKS AND NUNS AND VAMPIRES AND MONSTERS AND STRIPPERS AND THE LIVING DEAD.

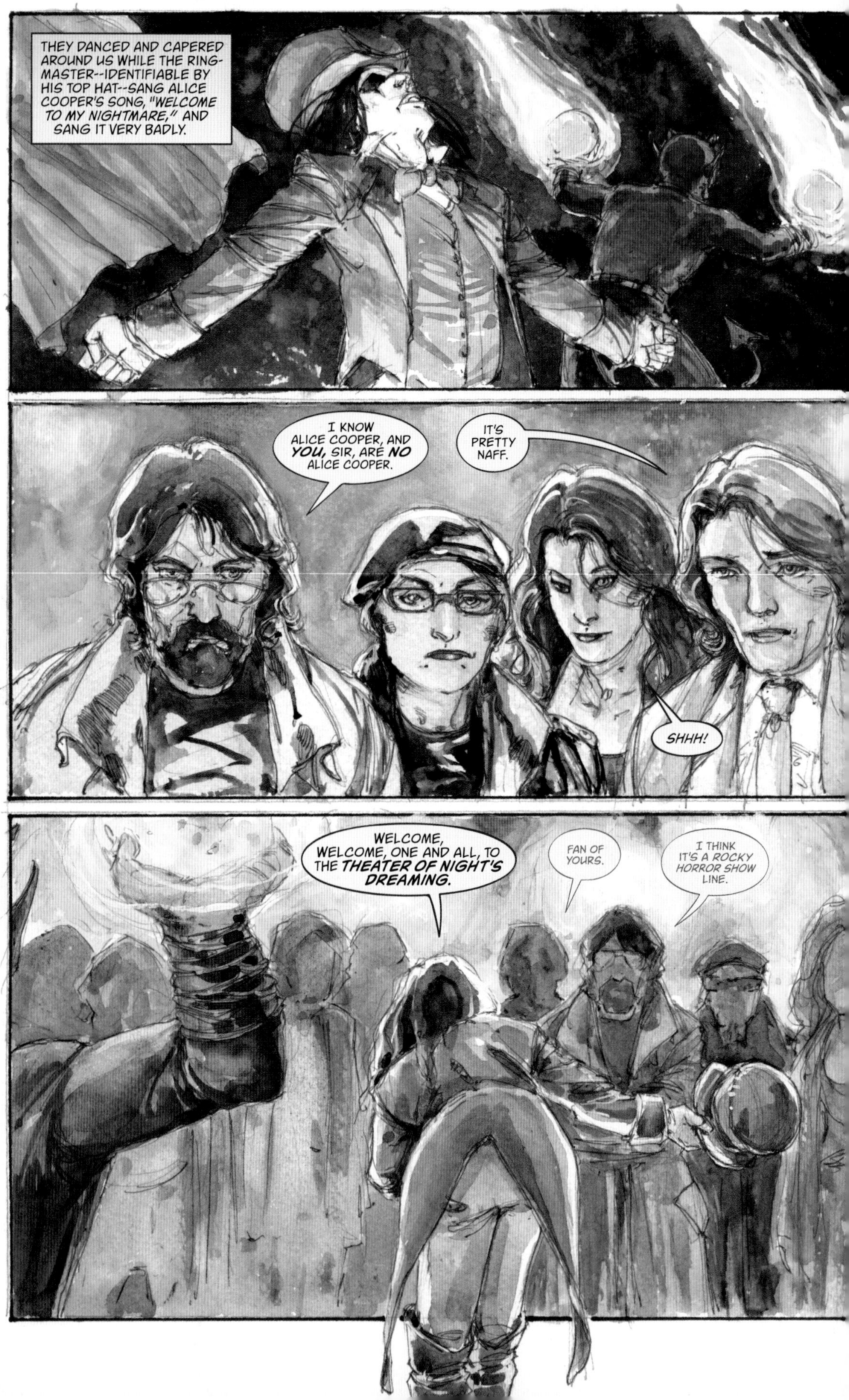

THEY DANCED AND CAPERED AROUND US WHILE THE RING-MASTER--IDENTIFIABLE BY HIS TOP HAT--SANG ALICE COOPER'S SONG, "WELCOME TO MY NIGHTMARE," AND SANG IT VERY BADLY.
I KNOW ALICE COOPER, AND YOU, SIR, ARE NO ALICE COOPER.
IT'S PRETTY NAFF.
SHHH!
WELCOME, WELCOME, ONE AND ALL, TO THE THEATER OF NIGHT'S DREAMING.
FAN OF YOURS.
I THINK IT'S A ROCKY HORROR SHOW LINE.

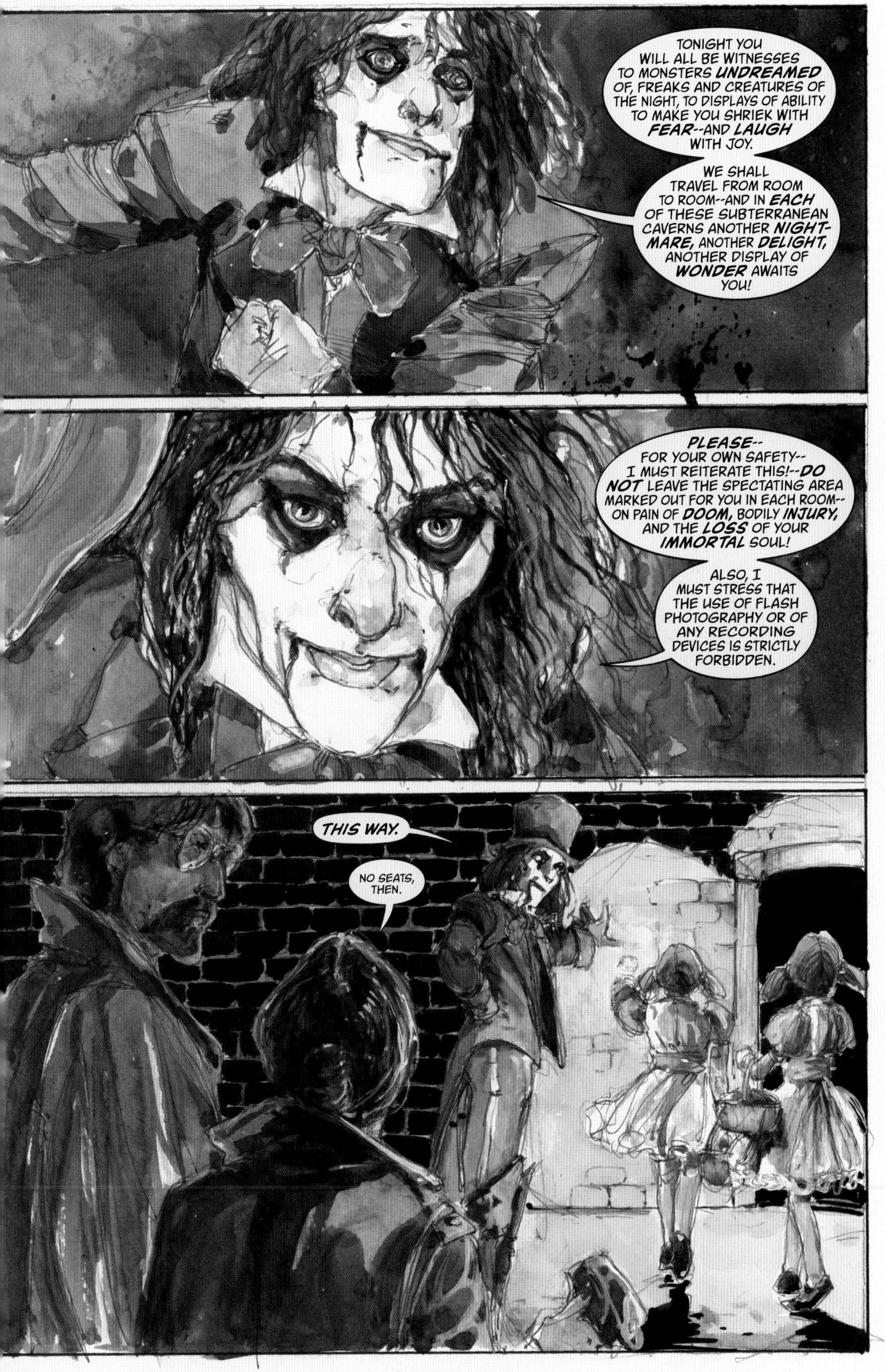
TONIGHT YOU WILL ALL BE WITNESSES TO MONSTERS UNDREAMED OF, FREAKS AND CREATURES OF THE NIGHT, TO DISPLAYS OF ABILITY TO MAKE YOU SHRIEK WITH FEAR--AND LAUGH WITH JOY.
WE SHALL TRAVEL FROM ROOM TO ROOM--AND IN EACH OF THESE SUBTERRANEAN CAVERNS ANOTHER NIGHT-MARE, ANOTHER DELIGHT, ANOTHER DISPLAY OF WONDER AWAITS YOU!
PLEASE-- FOR YOUR OWN SAFETY-- I MUST REITERATE THIS!--DO NOT LEAVE THE SPECTATING AREA MARKED OUT FOR YOU IN EACH ROOM--ON PAIN OF DOOM, BODILY INJURY, AND THE LOSS OF YOUR IMMORTAL SOUL!
ALSO, I MUST STRESS THAT THE USE OF FLASH PHOTOGRAPHY OR OF ANY RECORDING DEVICES IS STRICTLY FORBIDDEN.
THIS WAY.
NO SEATS, THEN.

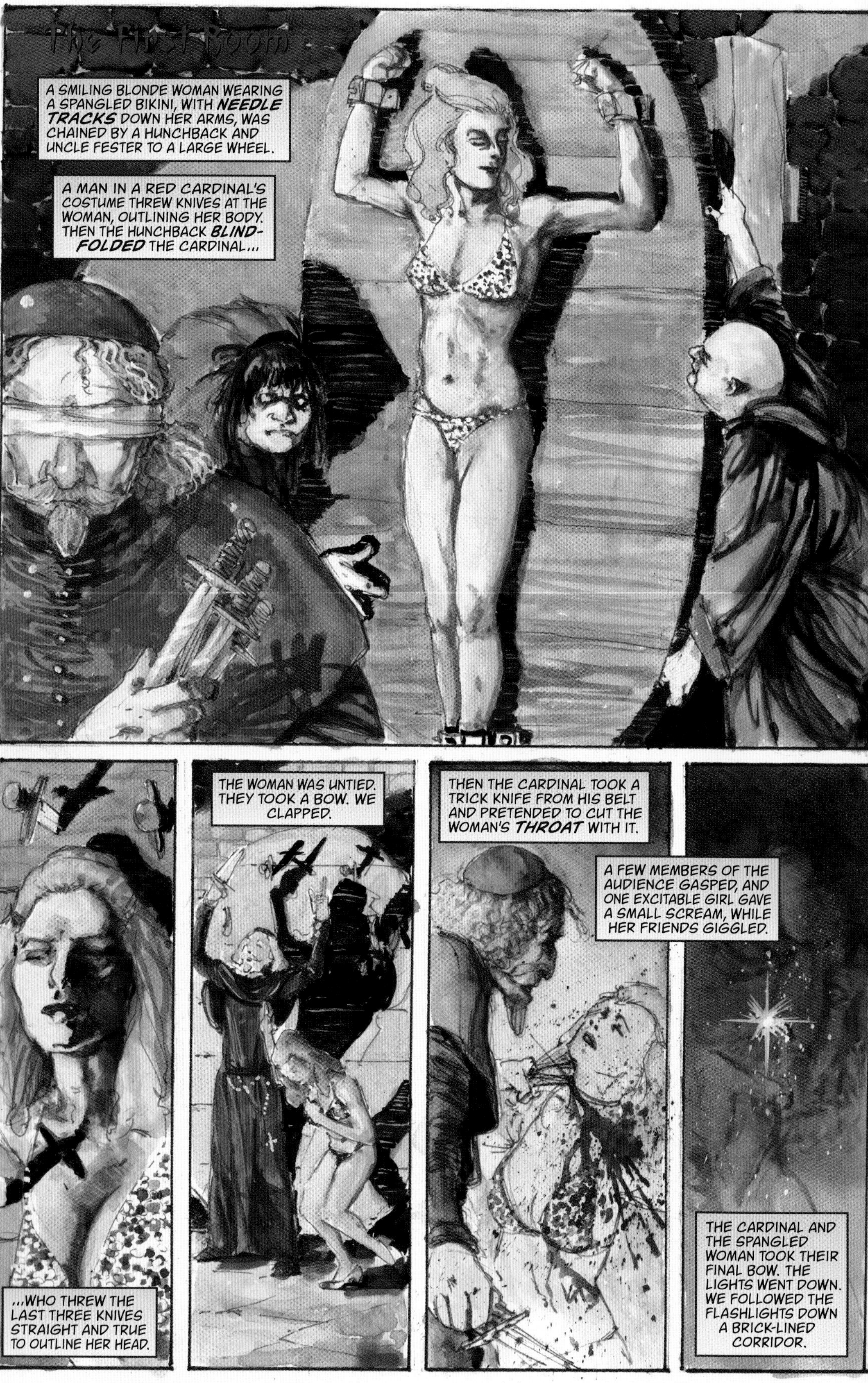

The First Room
A SMILING BLONDE WOMAN WEARING A SPANGLED BIKINI, WITH NEEDLE TRACKS DOWN HER ARMS, WAS CHAINED BY A HUNCHBACK AND UNCLE FESTER TO A LARGE WHEEL.
A MAN IN A RED CARDINAL'S COSTUME THREW KNIVES AT THE WOMAN, OUTLINING HER BODY. THEN THE HUNCHBACK BLIND-FOLDED THE CARDINAL...
...WHO THREW THE LAST THREE KNIVES STRAIGHT AND TRUE TO OUTLINE HER HEAD.
THE WOMAN WAS UNTIED. THEY TOOK A BOW. WE CLAPPED.
THEN THE CARDINAL TOOK A TRICK KNIFE FROM HIS BELT AND PRETENDED TO CUT THE WOMAN'S THROAT WITH IT.
A FEW MEMBERS OF THE AUDIENCE GASPED, AND ONE EXCITABLE GIRL GAVE A SMALL SCREAM, WHILE HER FRIENDS GIGGLED.
THE CARDINAL AND THE SPANGLED WOMAN TOOK THEIR FINAL BOW. THE LIGHTS WENT DOWN. WE FOLLOWED THE FLASHLIGHTS DOWN A BRICK-LINED CORRIDOR.

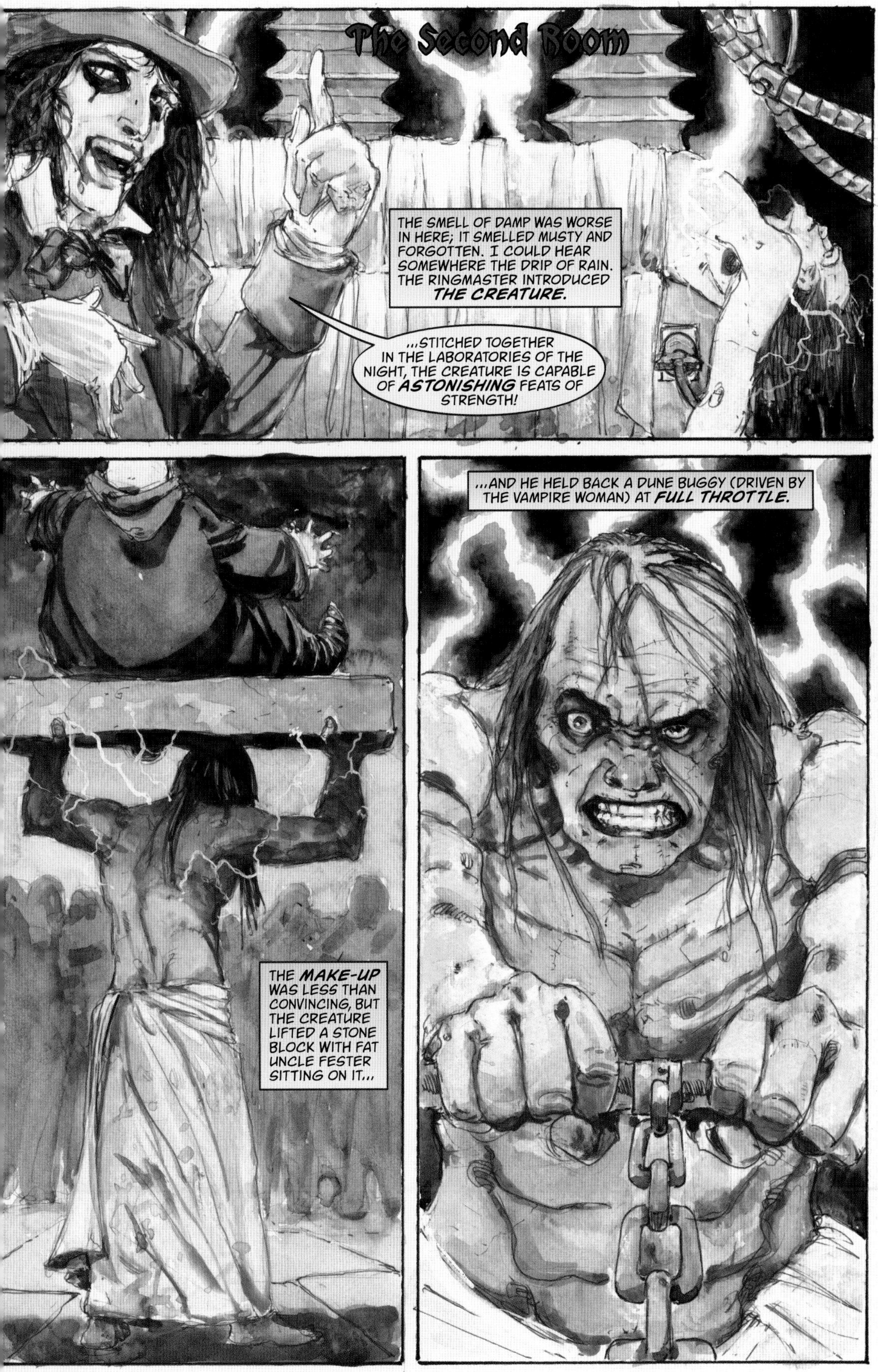
The Second Room
THE SMELL OF DAMP WAS WORSE IN HERE; IT SMELLED MUSTY AND FORGOTTEN. I COULD HEAR SOMEWHERE THE DRIP OF RAIN. THE RINGMASTER INTRODUCED THE CREATURE.
...STITCHED TOGETHER IN THE LABORATORIES OF THE NIGHT, THE CREATURE IS CAPABLE OF ASTONISHING FEATS OF STRENGTH!
THE MAKE-UP WAS LESS THAN CONVINCING, BUT THE CREATURE LIFTED A STONE BLOCK WITH FAT UNCLE FESTER SITTING ON IT...
...AND HE HELD BACK A DUNE BUGGY (DRIVEN BY THE VAMPIRE WOMAN) AT FULL THROTTLE.

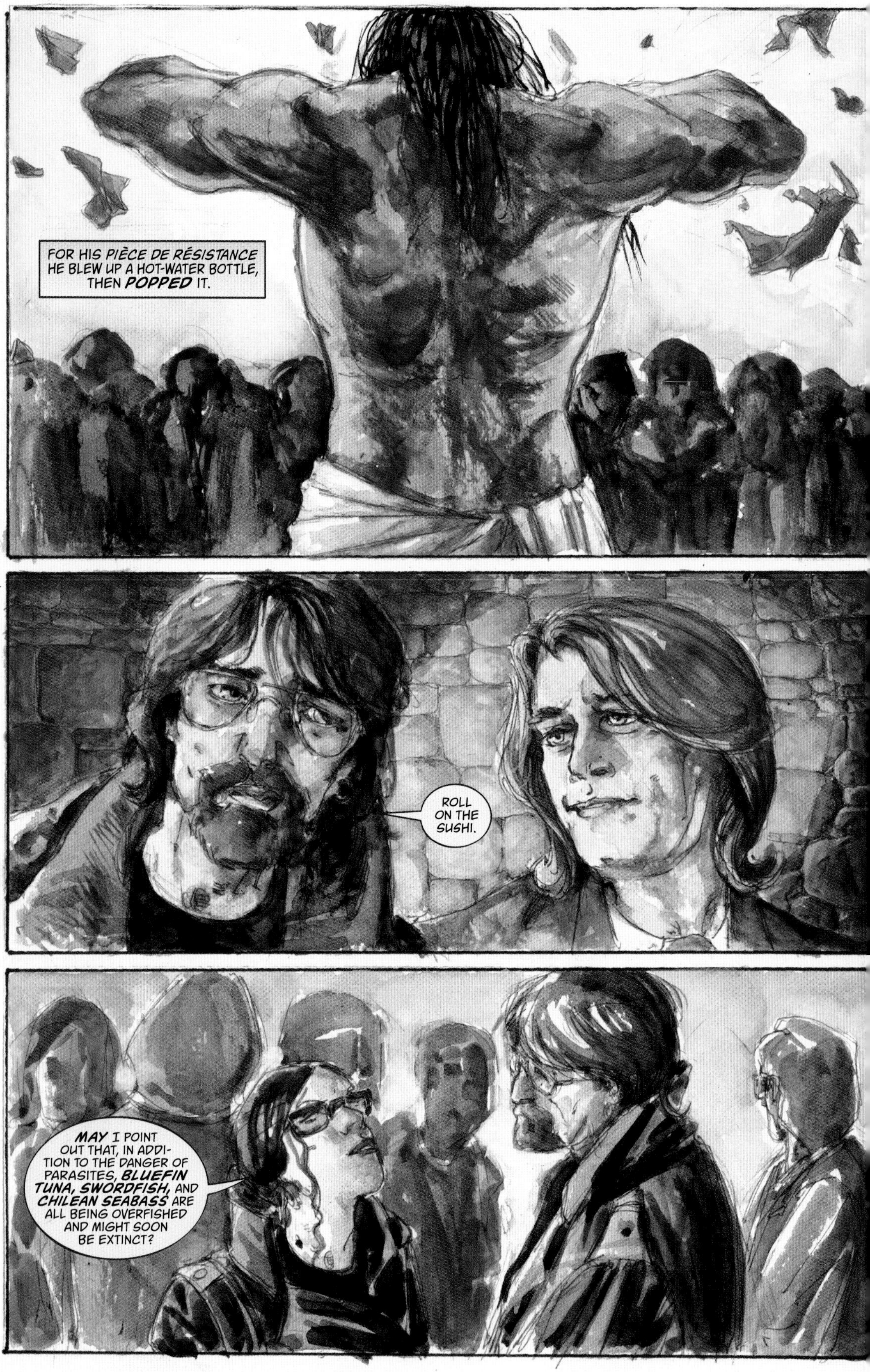
FOR HIS PIÈCE DE RÉSISTANCE HE BLEW UP A HOT-WATER BOTTLE, THEN POPPED IT.
ROLL ON THE SUSHI.
MAY I POINT OUT THAT, IN ADDITION TO THE DANGER OF PARASITES, BLUEFIN TUNA, SWORDFISH, AND CHILEAN SEABASS ARE ALL BEING OVERFISHED AND MIGHT SOON BE EXTINCT?

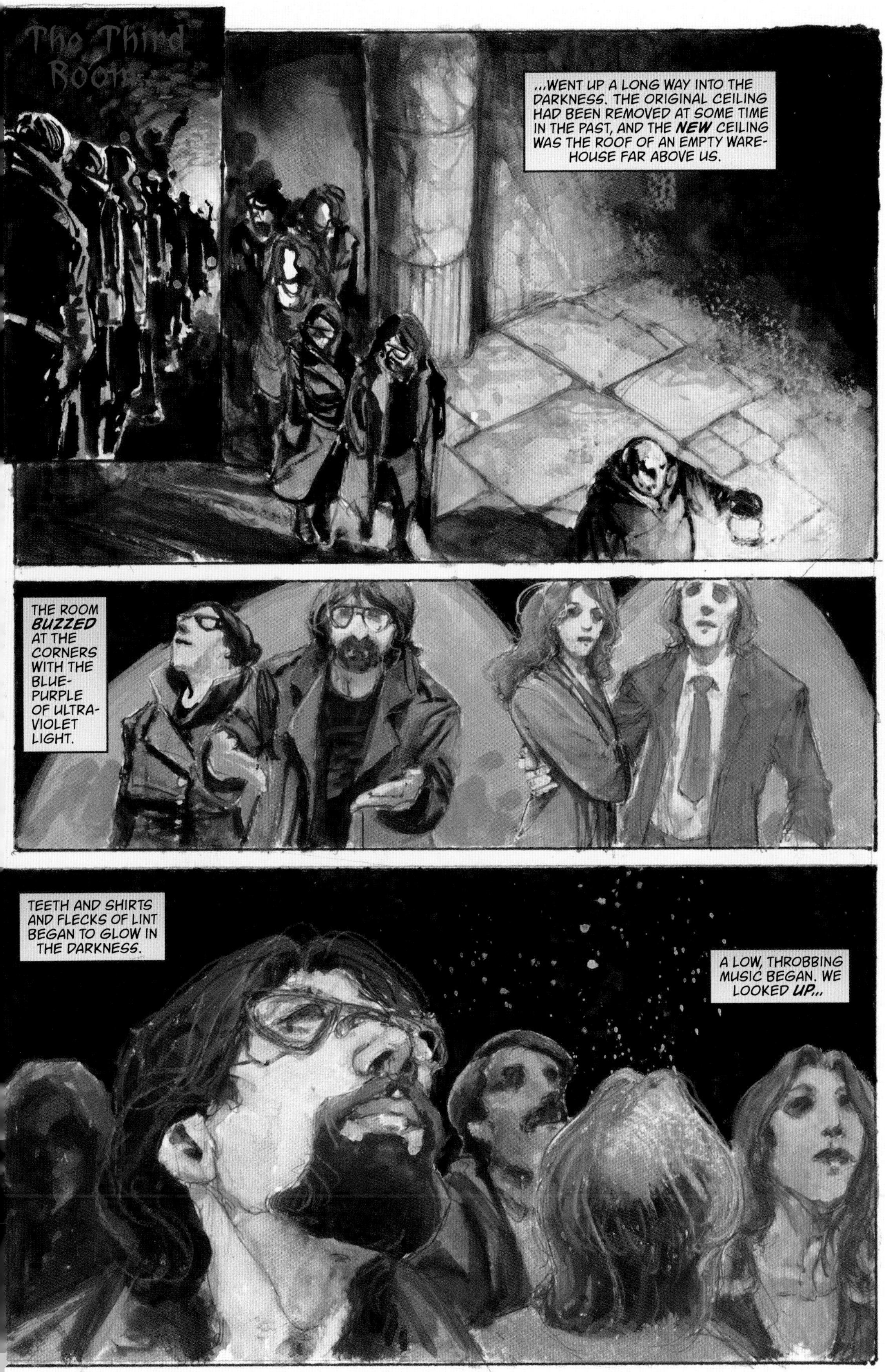
The Third Room
...WENT UP A LONG WAY INTO THE DARKNESS. THE ORIGINAL CEILING HAD BEEN REMOVED AT SOME TIME IN THE PAST, AND THE NEW CEILING WAS THE ROOF OF AN EMPTY WAREHOUSE FAR ABOVE US.
THE ROOM BUZZED AT THE CORNERS WITH THE BLUE-PURPLE OF ULTRA-VIOLET LIGHT.
TEETH AND SHIRTS AND FLECKS OF LINT BEGAN TO GLOW IN THE DARKNESS.
A LOW, THROBBING MUSIC BEGAN. WE LOOKED UP...

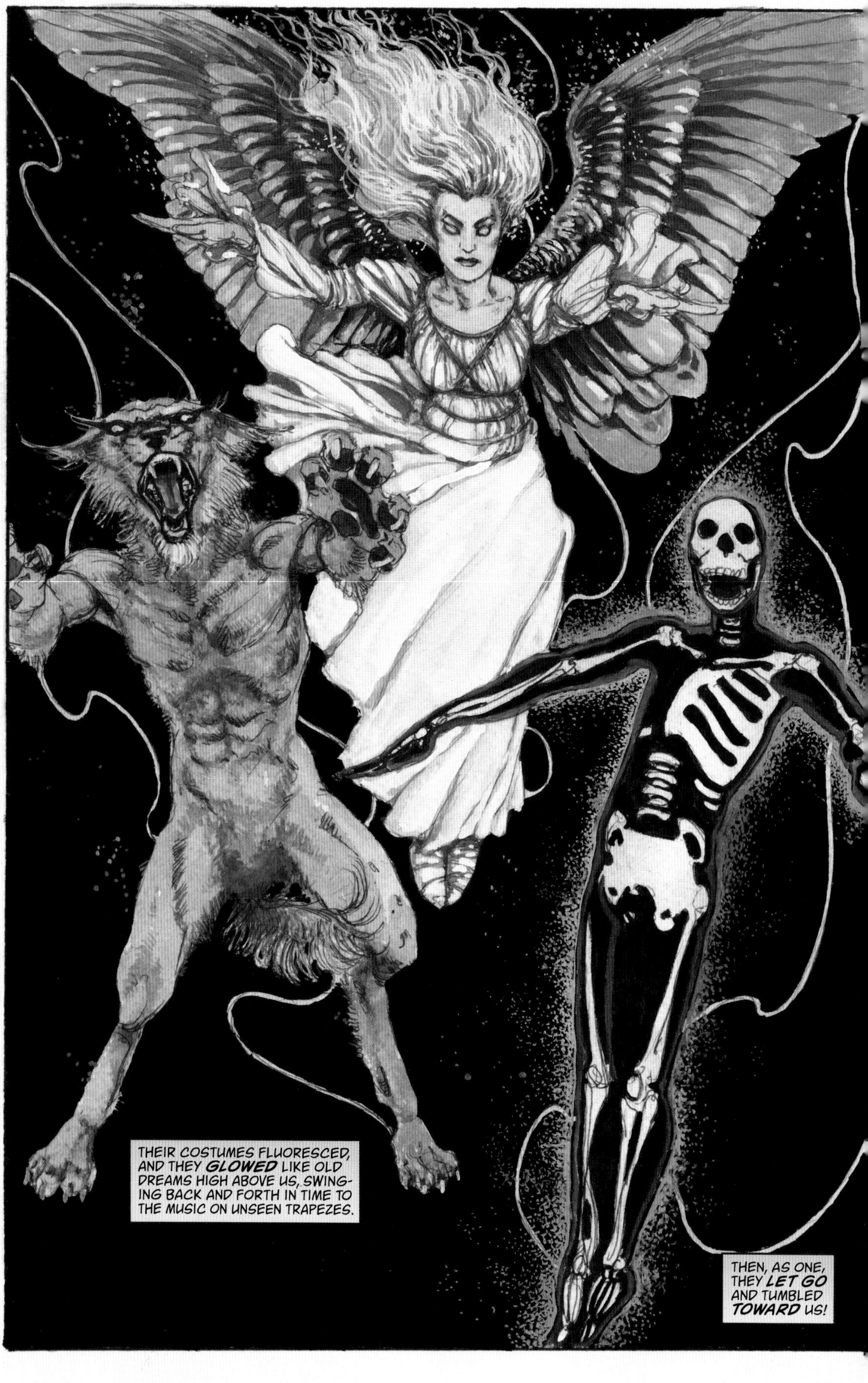
THEIR COSTUMES FLUORESCED, AND THEY **GLOWED** LIKE OLD DREAMS HIGH ABOVE US, SWINGING BACK AND FORTH IN TIME TO THE MUSIC ON UNSEEN TRAPEZES.
THEN, AS ONE, THEY **LET GO** AND TUMBLED **TOWARD** US!

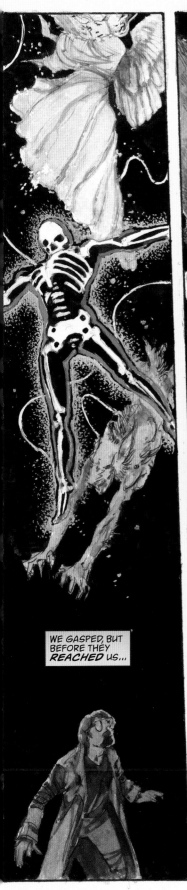

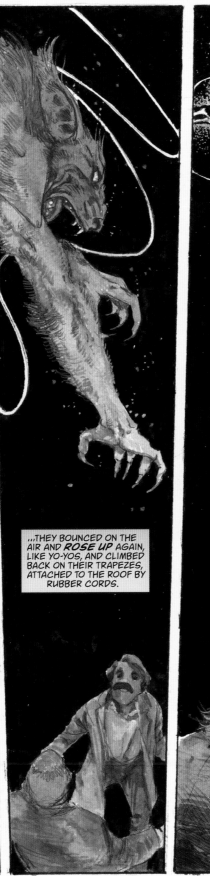

THEY BOUNCED AND DOVE AND *SWAM* THROUGH THE AIR ABOVE US WHILE WE CLAPPED AND GASPED AND WATCHED THEM IN HAPPY SILENCE.

...THEY BOUNCED ON THE AIR AND *ROSE UP* AGAIN, LIKE YO-YOS, AND CLIMBED BACK ON THEIR TRAPEZES, ATTACHED TO THE ROOF BY RUBBER CORDS.

WE GASPED, BUT BEFORE THEY *REACHED* US...

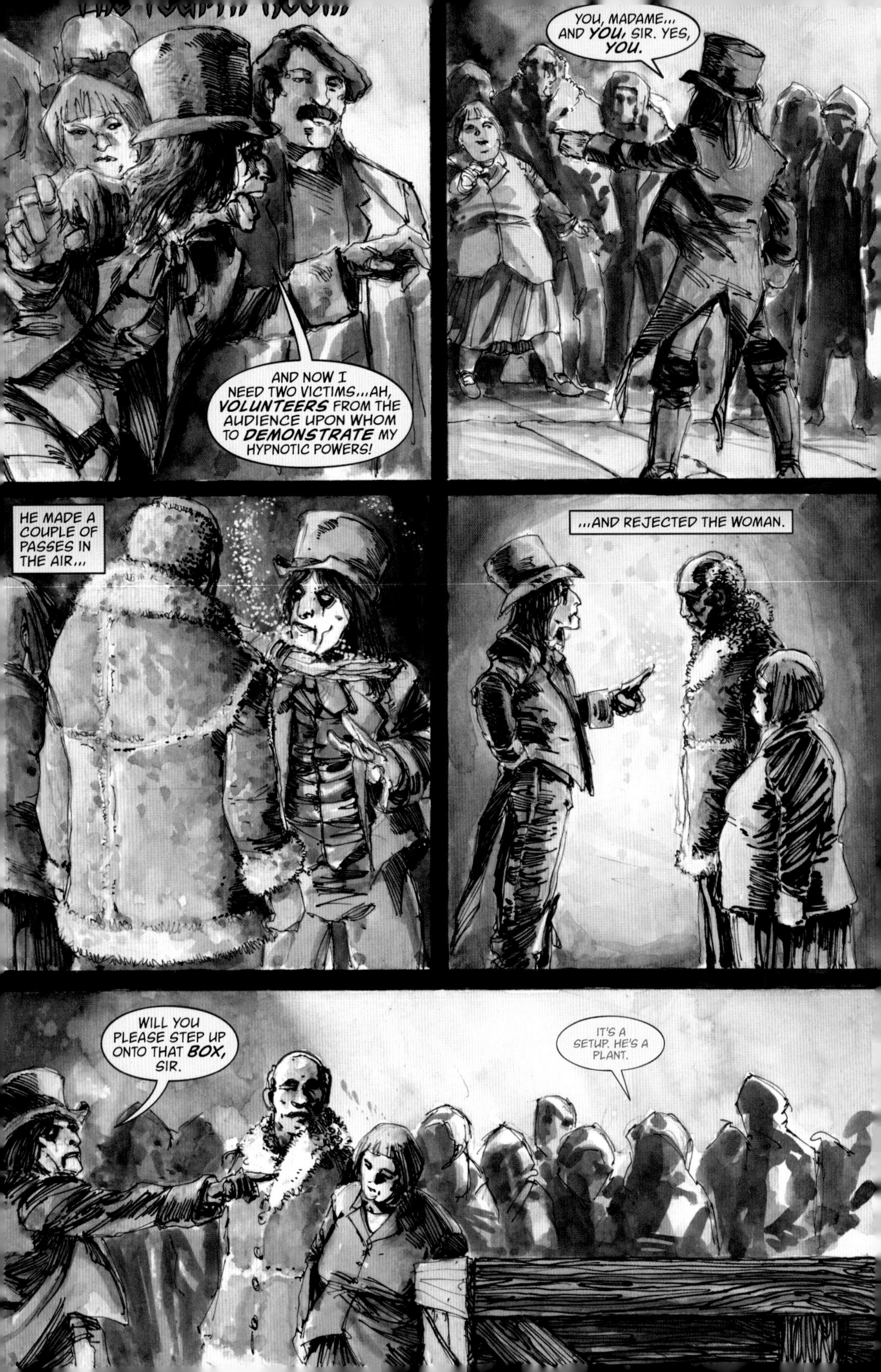
AND NOW I NEED TWO VICTIMS...AH, VOLUNTEERS FROM THE AUDIENCE UPON WHOM TO DEMONSTRATE MY HYPNOTIC POWERS!
YOU, MADAME... AND YOU, SIR. YES, YOU.
HE MADE A COUPLE OF PASSES IN THE AIR...
...AND REJECTED THE WOMAN.
WILL YOU PLEASE STEP UP ONTO THAT BOX, SIR.
IT'S A SETUP. HE'S A PLANT.

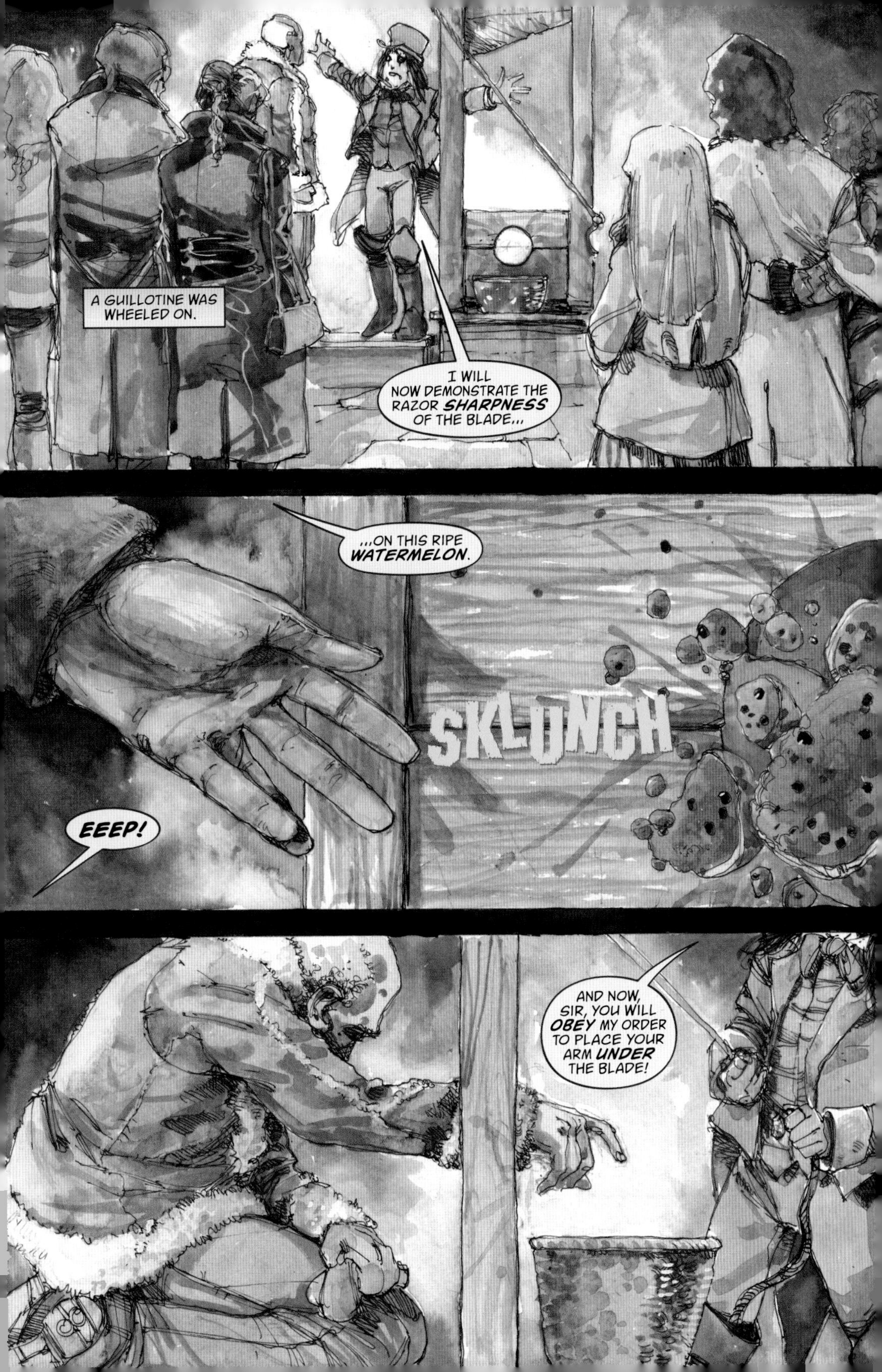
A GUILLOTINE WAS WHEELED ON.
I WILL NOW DEMONSTRATE THE RAZOR SHARPNESS OF THE BLADE...
...ON THIS RIPE WATERMELON.
SKLUNCH
EEEP!
AND NOW, SIR, YOU WILL OBEY MY ORDER TO PLACE YOUR ARM UNDER THE BLADE!

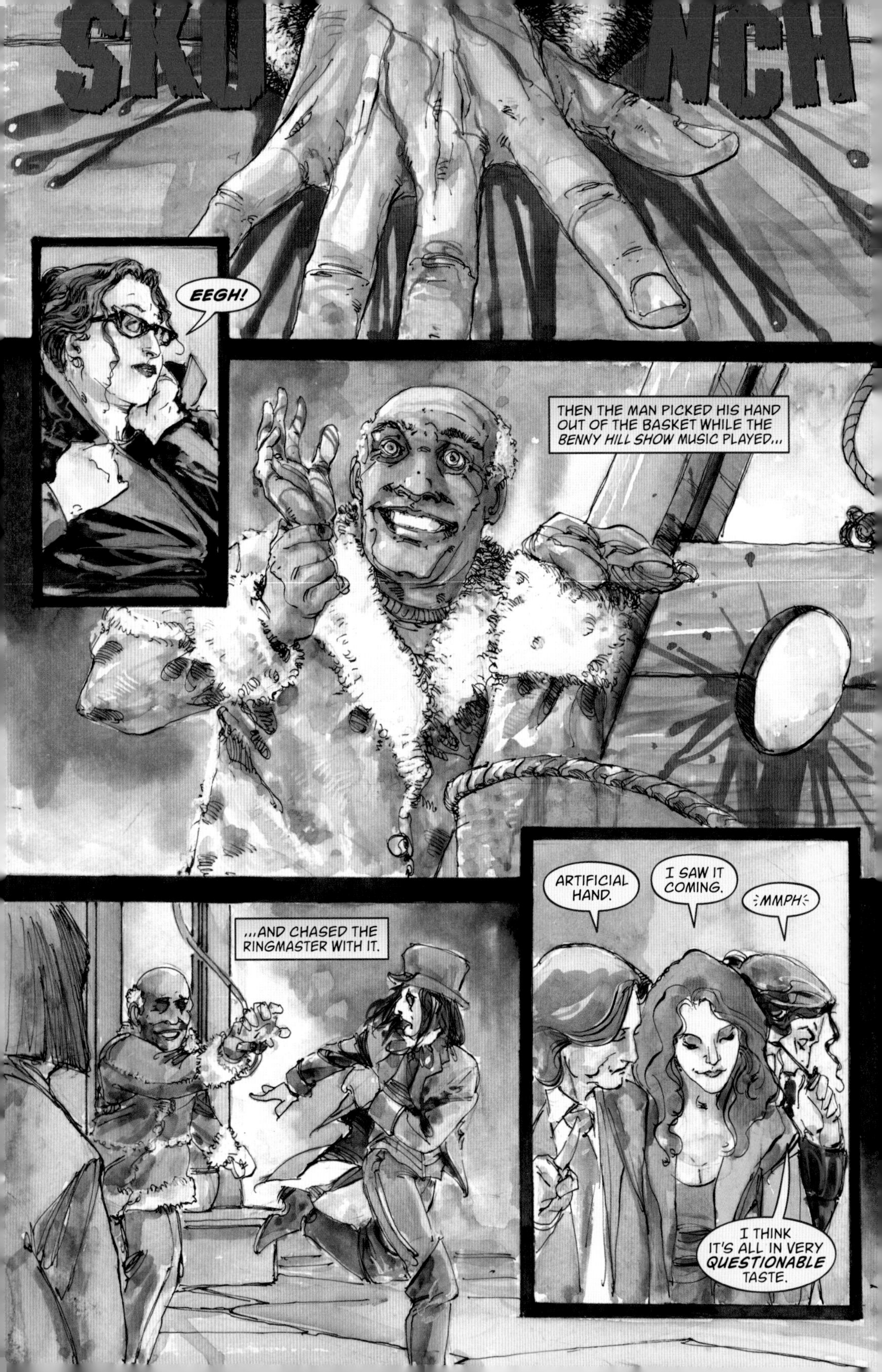
SKU NCH
EEGH!
THEN THE MAN PICKED HIS HAND OUT OF THE BASKET WHILE THE BENNY HILL SHOW MUSIC PLAYED...
...AND CHASED THE RINGMASTER WITH IT.
ARTIFICIAL HAND.
I SAW IT COMING.
MMPH
I THINK IT'S ALL IN VERY QUESTIONABLE TASTE.

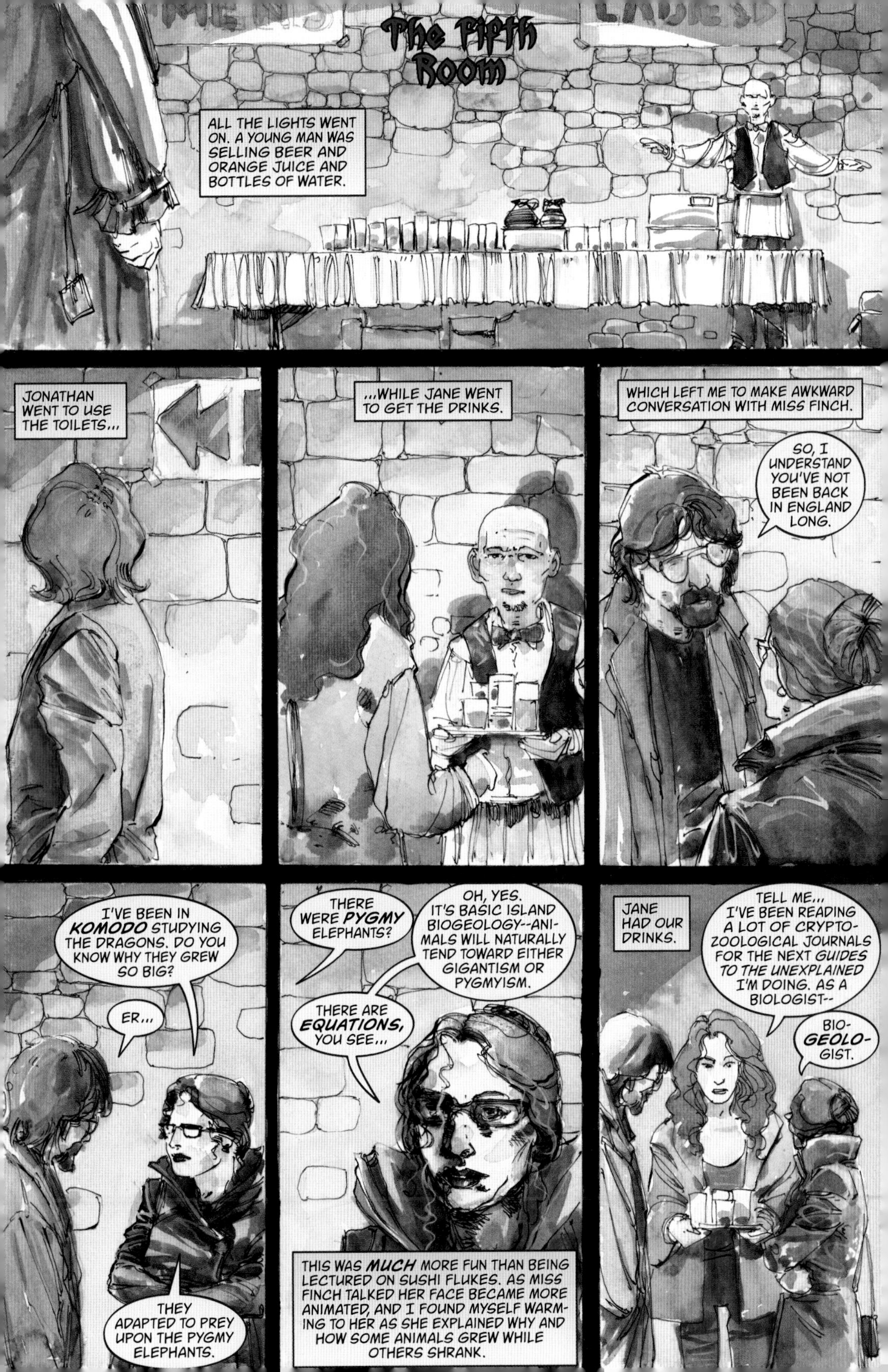
The Fifth Room
ALL THE LIGHTS WENT ON. A YOUNG MAN WAS SELLING BEER AND ORANGE JUICE AND BOTTLES OF WATER.
JONATHAN WENT TO USE THE TOILETS...
...WHILE JANE WENT TO GET THE DRINKS.
WHICH LEFT ME TO MAKE AWKWARD CONVERSATION WITH MISS FINCH.
SO, I UNDERSTAND YOU'VE NOT BEEN BACK IN ENGLAND LONG.
I'VE BEEN IN KOMODO STUDYING THE DRAGONS. DO YOU KNOW WHY THEY GREW SO BIG?
ER...
THEY ADAPTED TO PREY UPON THE PYGMY ELEPHANTS.
THERE WERE PYGMY ELEPHANTS?
OH, YES. IT'S BASIC ISLAND BIOGEOLOGY--ANIMALS WILL NATURALLY TEND TOWARD EITHER GIGANTISM OR PYGMYISM.
THERE ARE EQUATIONS, YOU SEE...
THIS WAS MUCH MORE FUN THAN BEING LECTURED ON SUSHI FLUKES. AS MISS FINCH TALKED HER FACE BECAME MORE ANIMATED, AND I FOUND MYSELF WARMING TO HER AS SHE EXPLAINED WHY AND HOW SOME ANIMALS GREW WHILE OTHERS SHRANK.
JANE HAD OUR DRINKS.
TELL ME... I'VE BEEN READING A LOT OF CRYPTOZOOLOGICAL JOURNALS FOR THE NEXT GUIDES TO THE UNEXPLAINED I'M DOING. AS A BIOLOGIST--
BIO-GEOLO-GIST.

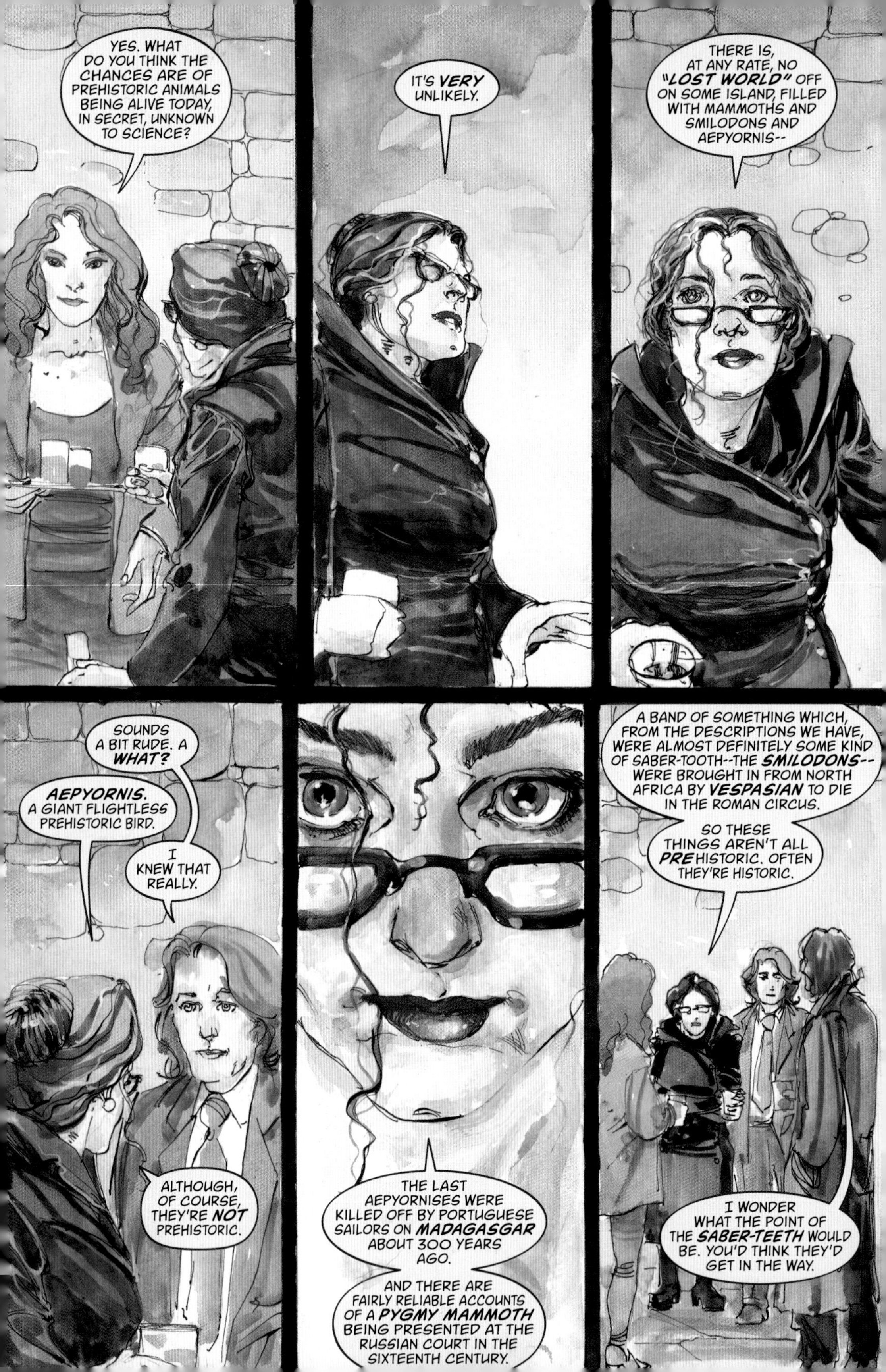
YES. WHAT DO YOU THINK THE CHANCES ARE OF PREHISTORIC ANIMALS BEING ALIVE TODAY, IN SECRET, UNKNOWN TO SCIENCE?
IT'S VERY UNLIKELY.
THERE IS, AT ANY RATE, NO "LOST WORLD" OFF ON SOME ISLAND, FILLED WITH MAMMOTHS AND SMILODONS AND AEPYORNIS--
SOUNDS A BIT RUDE. A WHAT?
AEPYORNIS. A GIANT FLIGHTLESS PREHISTORIC BIRD.
I KNEW THAT REALLY.
ALTHOUGH, OF COURSE, THEY'RE NOT PREHISTORIC.
THE LAST AEPYORNISES WERE KILLED OFF BY PORTUGUESE SAILORS ON MADAGASGAR ABOUT 300 YEARS AGO.
AND THERE ARE FAIRLY RELIABLE ACCOUNTS OF A PYGMY MAMMOTH BEING PRESENTED AT THE RUSSIAN COURT IN THE SIXTEENTH CENTURY.
A BAND OF SOMETHING WHICH, FROM THE DESCRIPTIONS WE HAVE, WERE ALMOST DEFINITELY SOME KIND OF SABER-TOOTH--THE SMILODONS--WERE BROUGHT IN FROM NORTH AFRICA BY VESPASIAN TO DIE IN THE ROMAN CIRCUS.
SO THESE THINGS AREN'T ALL PREHISTORIC. OFTEN THEY'RE HISTORIC.
I WONDER WHAT THE POINT OF THE SABER-TEETH WOULD BE. YOU'D THINK THEY'D GET IN THE WAY.

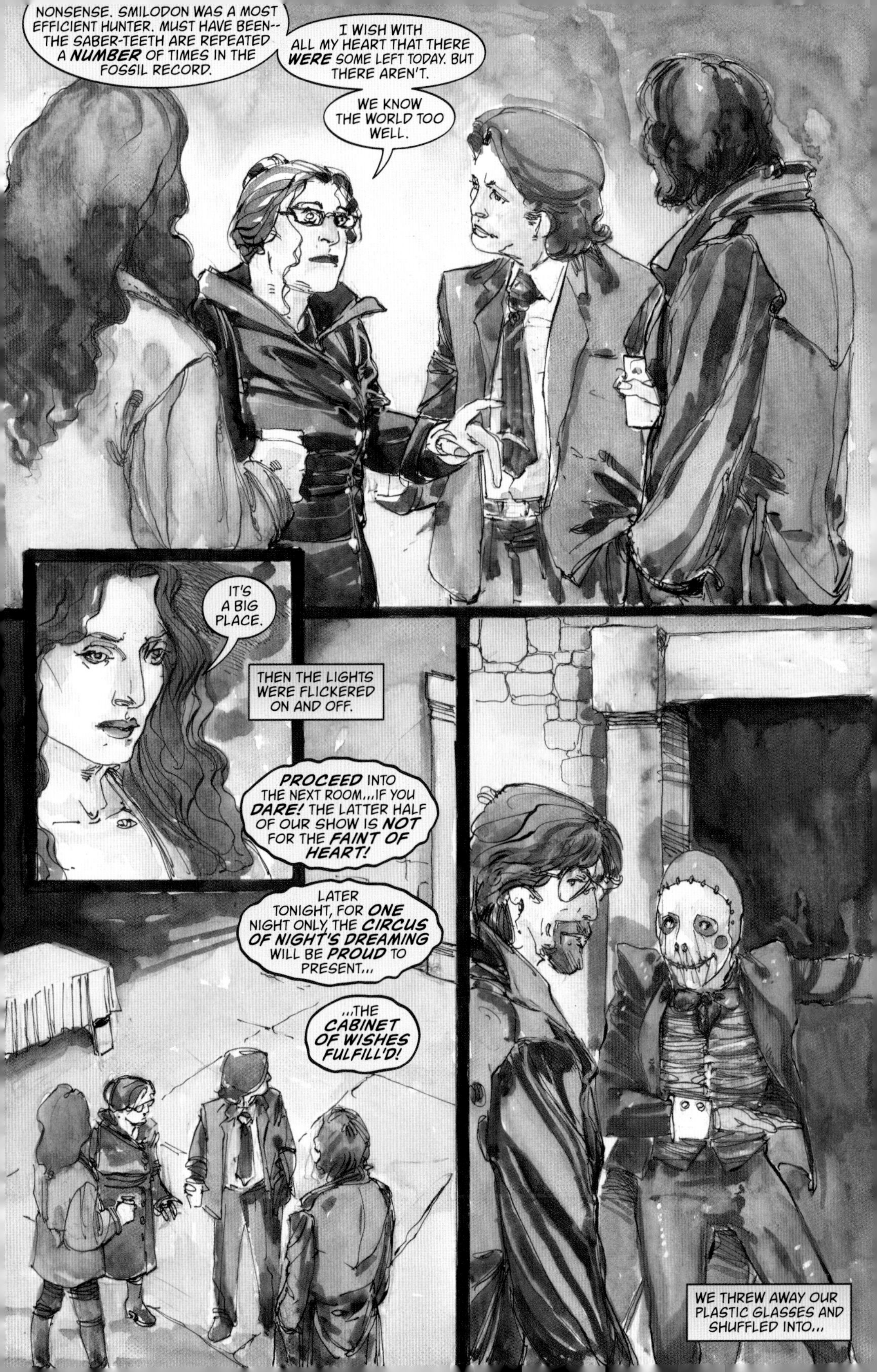
NONSENSE. SMILODON WAS A MOST EFFICIENT HUNTER. MUST HAVE BEEN-- THE SABER-TEETH ARE REPEATED A NUMBER OF TIMES IN THE FOSSIL RECORD.
I WISH WITH ALL MY HEART THAT THERE WERE SOME LEFT TODAY. BUT THERE AREN'T.
WE KNOW THE WORLD TOO WELL.
IT'S A BIG PLACE.
THEN THE LIGHTS WERE FLICKERED ON AND OFF.
PROCEED INTO THE NEXT ROOM...IF YOU DARE! THE LATTER HALF OF OUR SHOW IS NOT FOR THE FAINT OF HEART!
LATER TONIGHT, FOR ONE NIGHT ONLY, THE CIRCUS OF NIGHT'S DREAMING WILL BE PROUD TO PRESENT...
...THE CABINET OF WISHES FULFILL'D!
WE THREW AWAY OUR PLASTIC GLASSES AND SHUFFLED INTO...

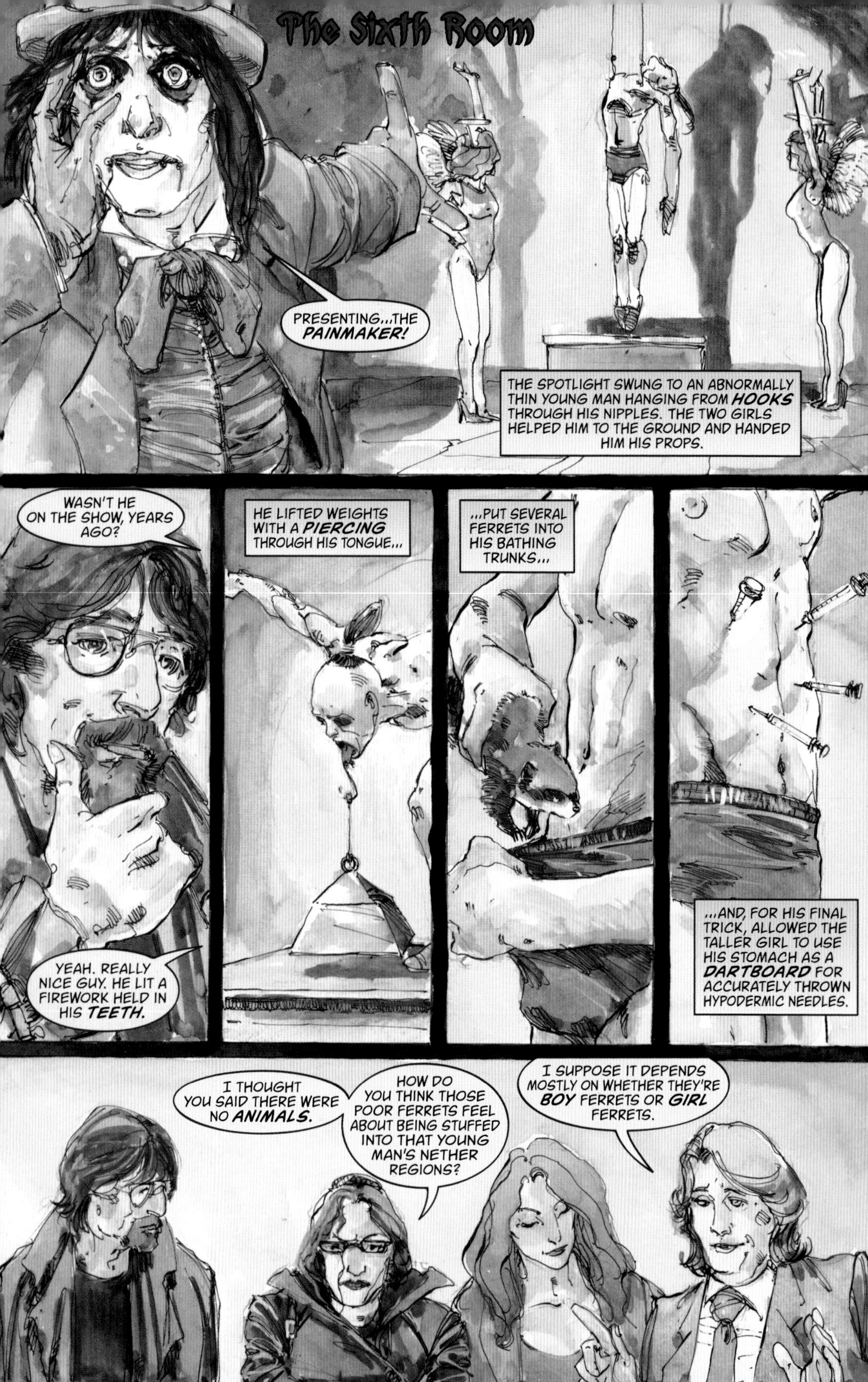
The Sixth Room
PRESENTING...THE PAINMAKER!
THE SPOTLIGHT SWUNG TO AN ABNORMALLY THIN YOUNG MAN HANGING FROM HOOKS THROUGH HIS NIPPLES. THE TWO GIRLS HELPED HIM TO THE GROUND AND HANDED HIM HIS PROPS.
WASN'T HE ON THE SHOW, YEARS AGO?
YEAH. REALLY NICE GUY. HE LIT A FIREWORK HELD IN HIS TEETH.
HE LIFTED WEIGHTS WITH A PIERCING THROUGH HIS TONGUE...
...PUT SEVERAL FERRETS INTO HIS BATHING TRUNKS...
...AND, FOR HIS FINAL TRICK, ALLOWED THE TALLER GIRL TO USE HIS STOMACH AS A DARTBOARD FOR ACCURATELY THROWN HYPODERMIC NEEDLES.
I THOUGHT YOU SAID THERE WERE NO ANIMALS.
HOW DO YOU THINK THOSE POOR FERRETS FEEL ABOUT BEING STUFFED INTO THAT YOUNG MAN'S NETHER REGIONS?
I SUPPOSE IT DEPENDS MOSTLY ON WHETHER THEY'RE BOY FERRETS OR GIRL FERRETS.

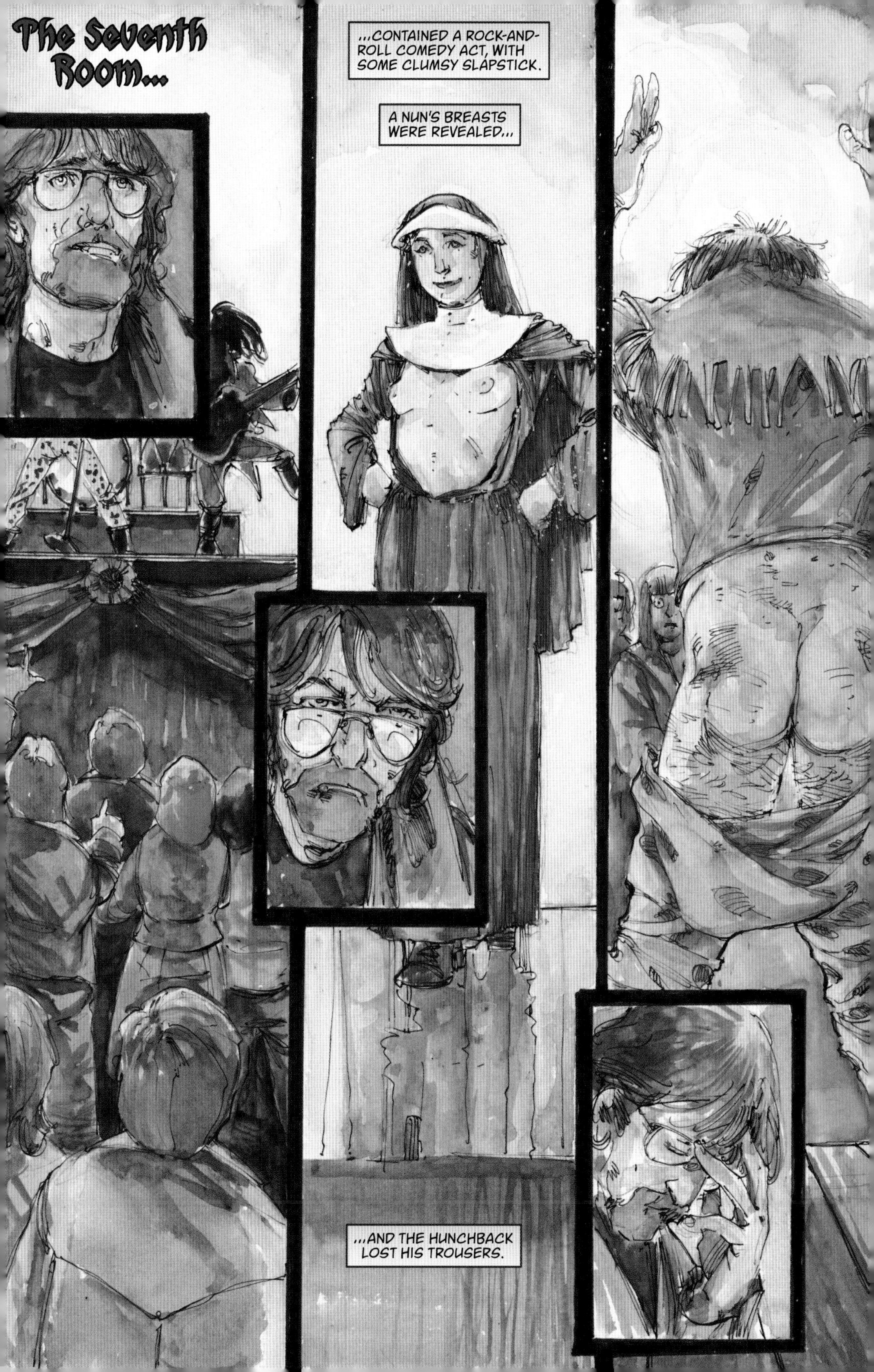
The Seventh Room...
...CONTAINED A ROCK-AND-ROLL COMEDY ACT, WITH SOME CLUMSY SLAPSTICK.
A NUN'S BREASTS WERE REVEALED...
...AND THE HUNCHBACK LOST HIS TROUSERS.

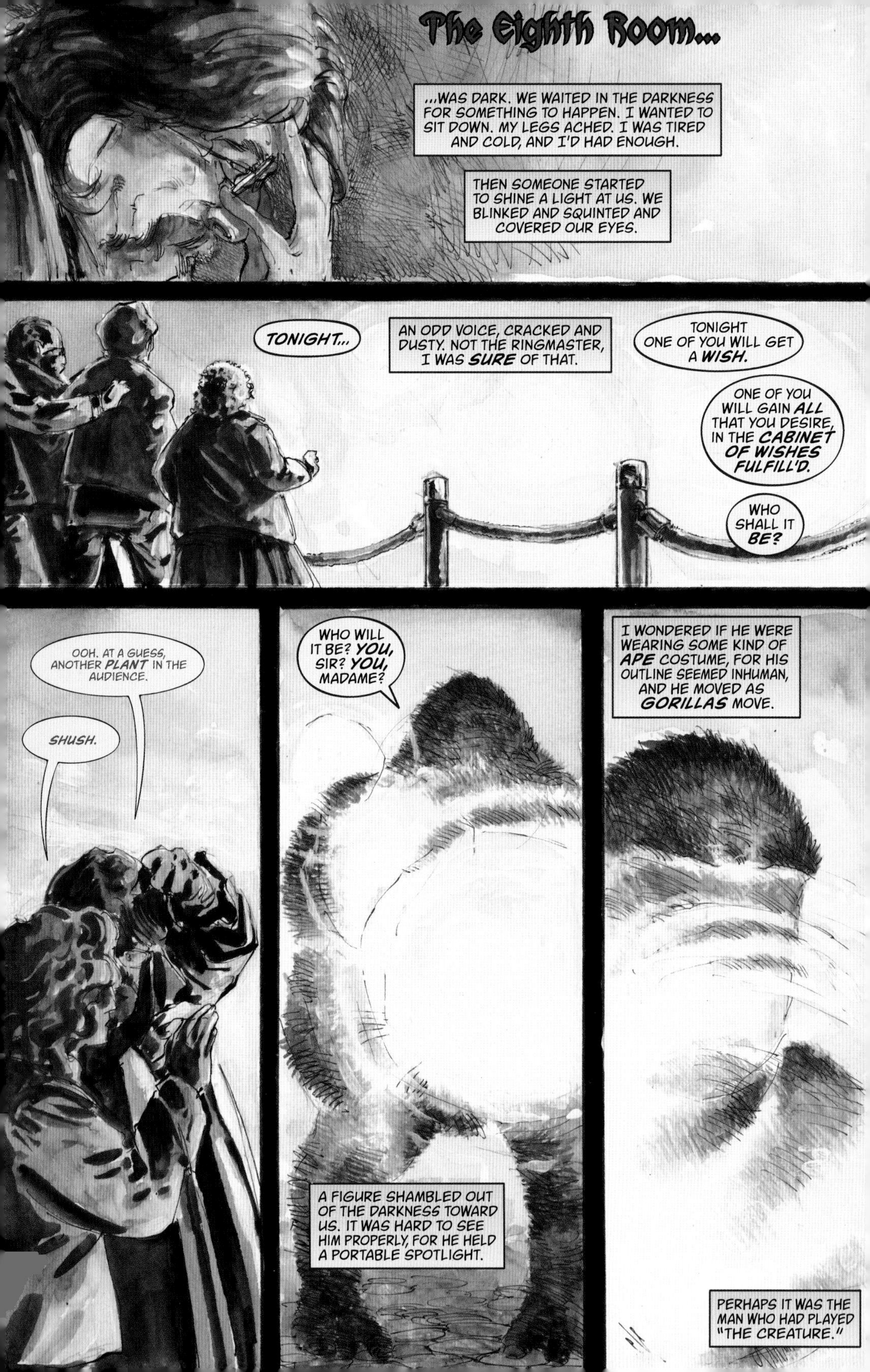
The Eighth Room...
...WAS DARK. WE WAITED IN THE DARKNESS FOR SOMETHING TO HAPPEN. I WANTED TO SIT DOWN. MY LEGS ACHED. I WAS TIRED AND COLD, AND I'D HAD ENOUGH.
THEN SOMEONE STARTED TO SHINE A LIGHT AT US. WE BLINKED AND SQUINTED AND COVERED OUR EYES.
TONIGHT...
AN ODD VOICE, CRACKED AND DUSTY. NOT THE RINGMASTER, I WAS SURE OF THAT.
TONIGHT ONE OF YOU WILL GET A WISH.
ONE OF YOU WILL GAIN ALL THAT YOU DESIRE, IN THE CABINET OF WISHES FULFILL'D.
WHO SHALL IT BE?
OOH. AT A GUESS, ANOTHER PLANT IN THE AUDIENCE.
SHUSH.
WHO WILL IT BE? YOU, SIR? YOU, MADAME?
A FIGURE SHAMBLED OUT OF THE DARKNESS TOWARD US. IT WAS HARD TO SEE HIM PROPERLY, FOR HE HELD A PORTABLE SPOTLIGHT.
I WONDERED IF HE WERE WEARING SOME KIND OF APE COSTUME, FOR HIS OUTLINE SEEMED INHUMAN, AND HE MOVED AS GORILLAS MOVE.
PERHAPS IT WAS THE MAN WHO HAD PLAYED "THE CREATURE."

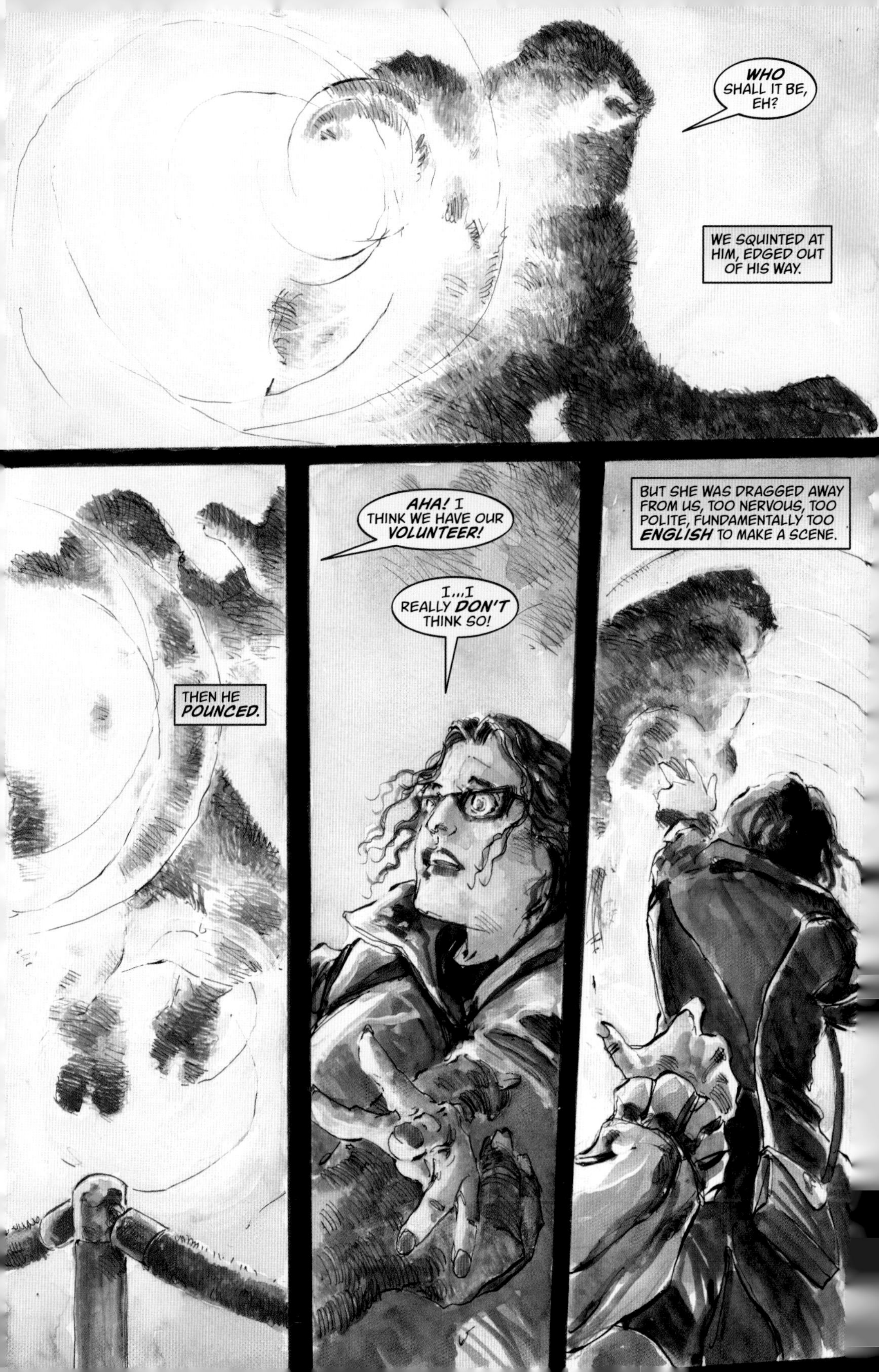
WHO SHALL IT BE, EH?
WE SQUINTED AT HIM, EDGED OUT OF HIS WAY.
THEN HE POUNCED.
AHA! I THINK WE HAVE OUR VOLUNTEER!
I...I REALLY DON'T THINK SO!
BUT SHE WAS DRAGGED AWAY FROM US, TOO NERVOUS, TOO POLITE, FUNDAMENTALLY TOO ENGLISH TO MAKE A SCENE.

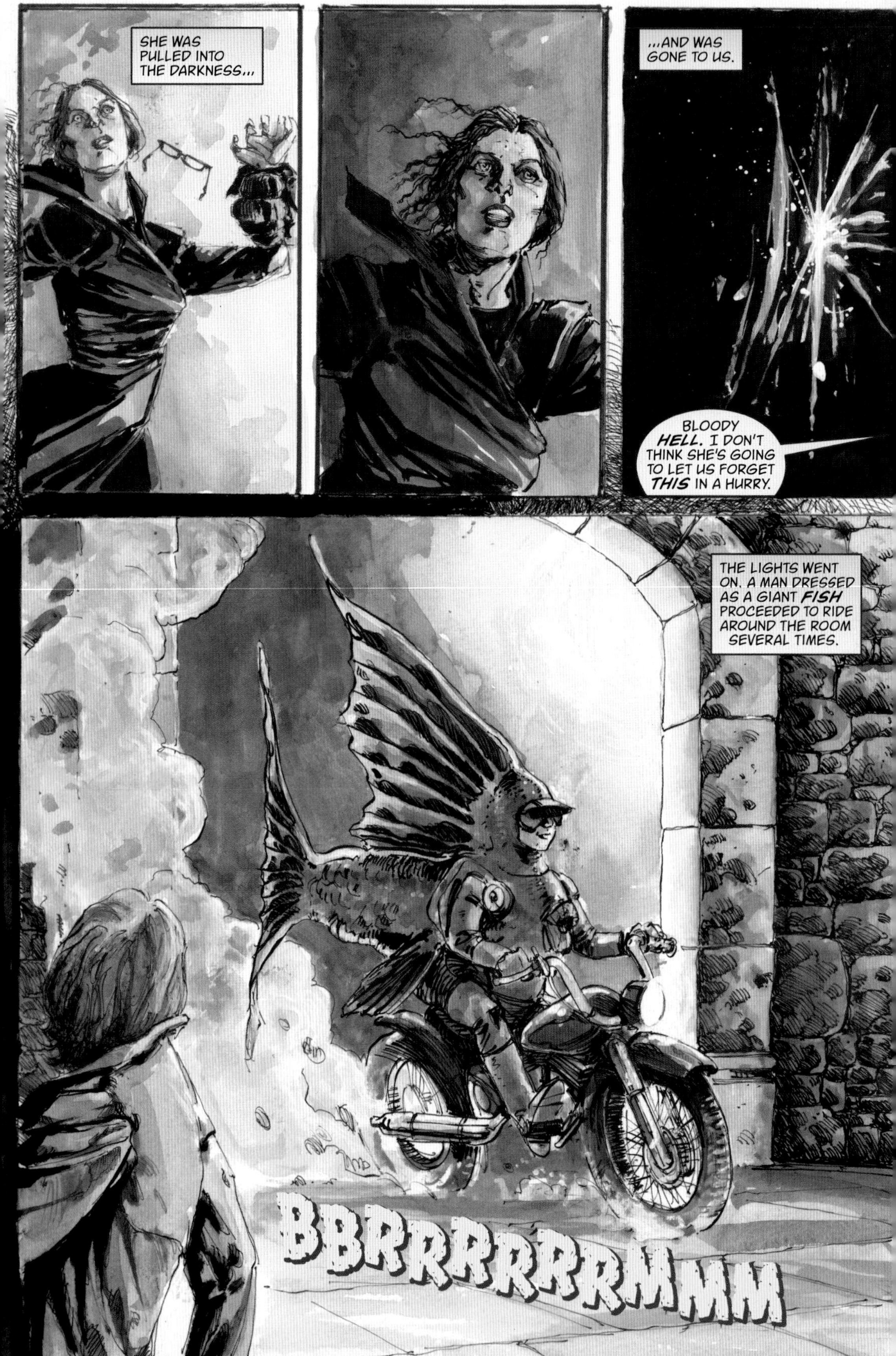

SHE WAS PULLED INTO THE DARKNESS...
...AND WAS GONE TO US.
BLOODY HELL. I DON'T THINK SHE'S GOING TO LET US FORGET THIS IN A HURRY.
THE LIGHTS WENT ON. A MAN DRESSED AS A GIANT FISH PROCEEDED TO RIDE AROUND THE ROOM SEVERAL TIMES.
BBRRRRRRRMMMM

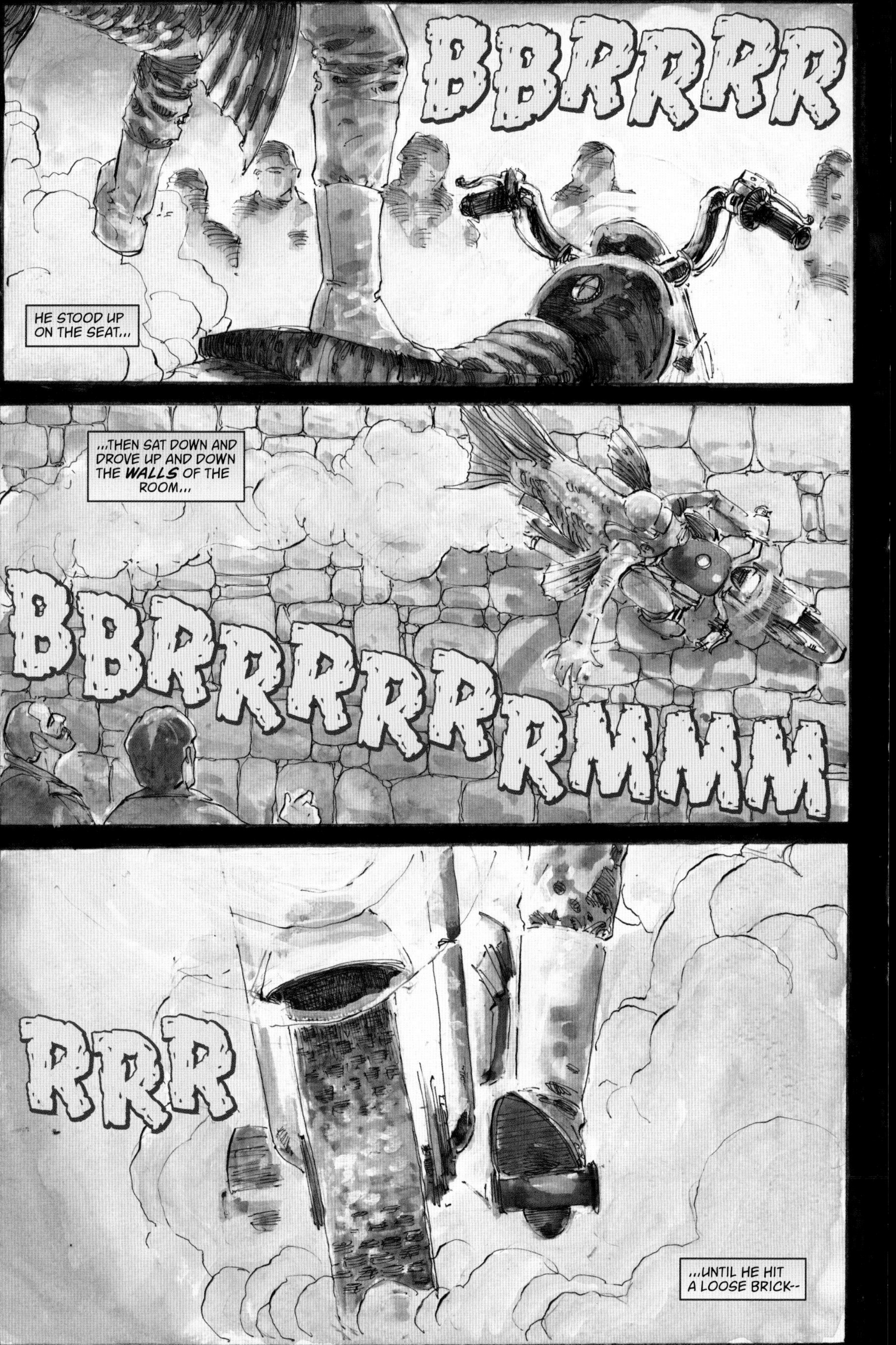
BBRRRRR
HE STOOD UP ON THE SEAT...
...THEN SAT DOWN AND DROVE UP AND DOWN THE WALLS OF THE ROOM...
BBRRRRRRMMMM
RRR
...UNTIL HE HIT A LOOSE BRICK--

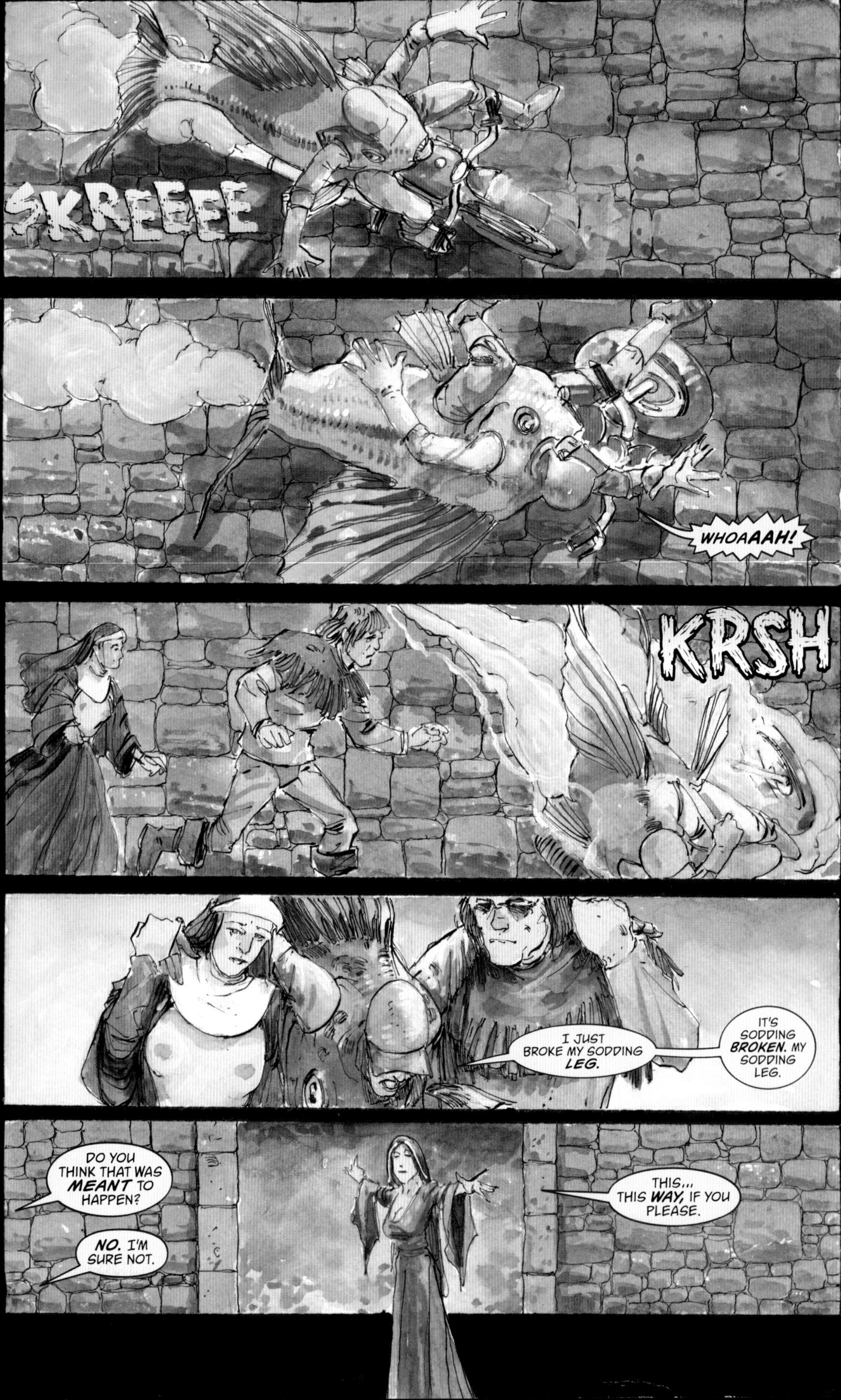
SKREEEE
WHOAAAH!
KRSH
I JUST BROKE MY SODDING LEG.
IT'S SODDING BROKEN. MY SODDING LEG.
DO YOU THINK THAT WAS MEANT TO HAPPEN?
NO. I'M SURE NOT.
THIS... THIS WAY, IF YOU PLEASE.

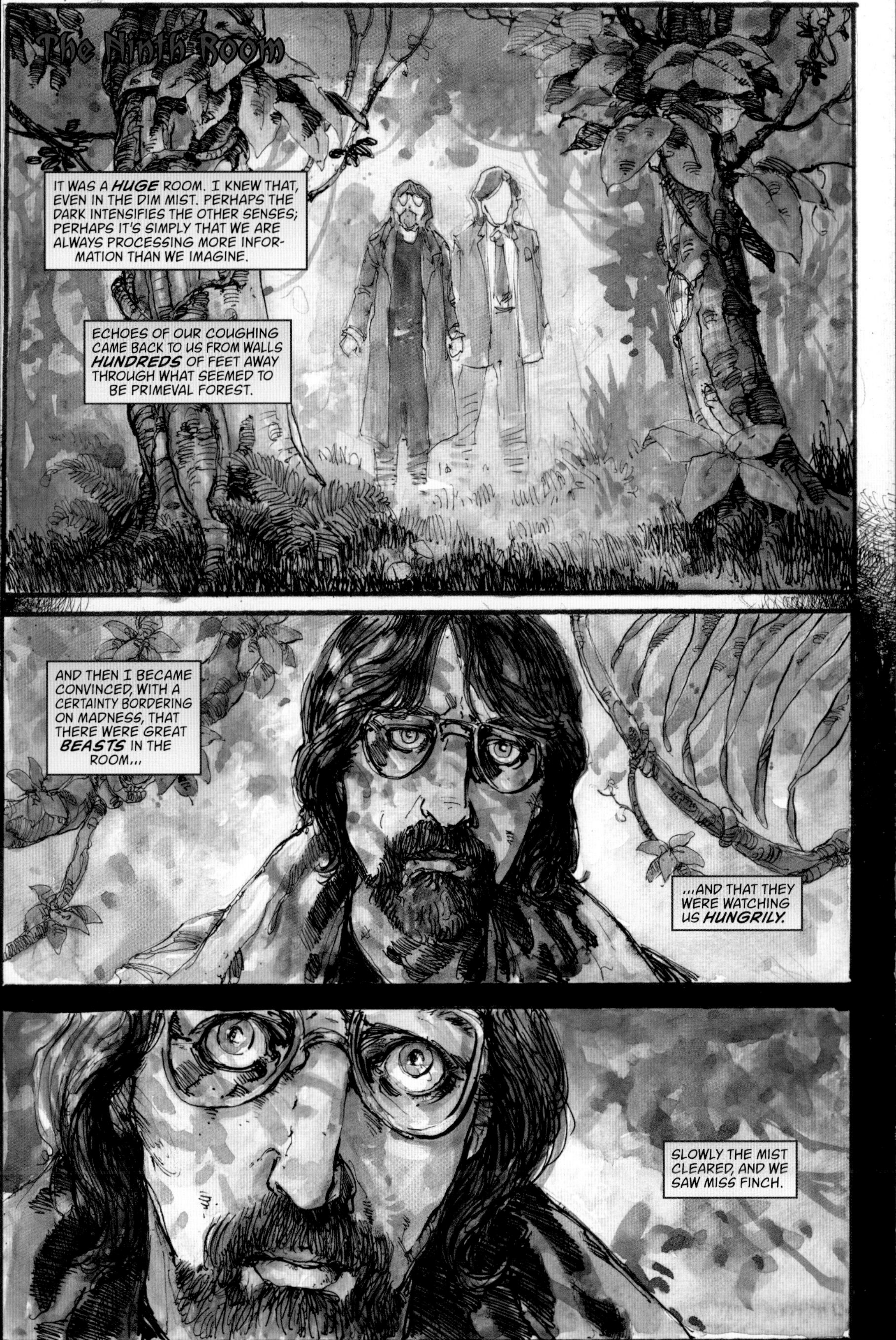
The Ninth Room
IT WAS A *HUGE* ROOM. I KNEW THAT, EVEN IN THE DIM MIST. PERHAPS THE DARK INTENSIFIES THE OTHER SENSES; PERHAPS IT'S SIMPLY THAT WE ARE ALWAYS PROCESSING MORE INFORMATION THAN WE IMAGINE.
ECHOES OF OUR COUGHING CAME BACK TO US FROM WALLS *HUNDREDS* OF FEET AWAY THROUGH WHAT SEEMED TO BE PRIMEVAL FOREST.
AND THEN I BECAME CONVINCED, WITH A CERTAINTY BORDERING ON MADNESS, THAT THERE WERE GREAT *BEASTS* IN THE ROOM...
...AND THAT THEY WERE WATCHING US *HUNGRILY.*
SLOWLY THE MIST CLEARED, AND WE SAW MISS FINCH.

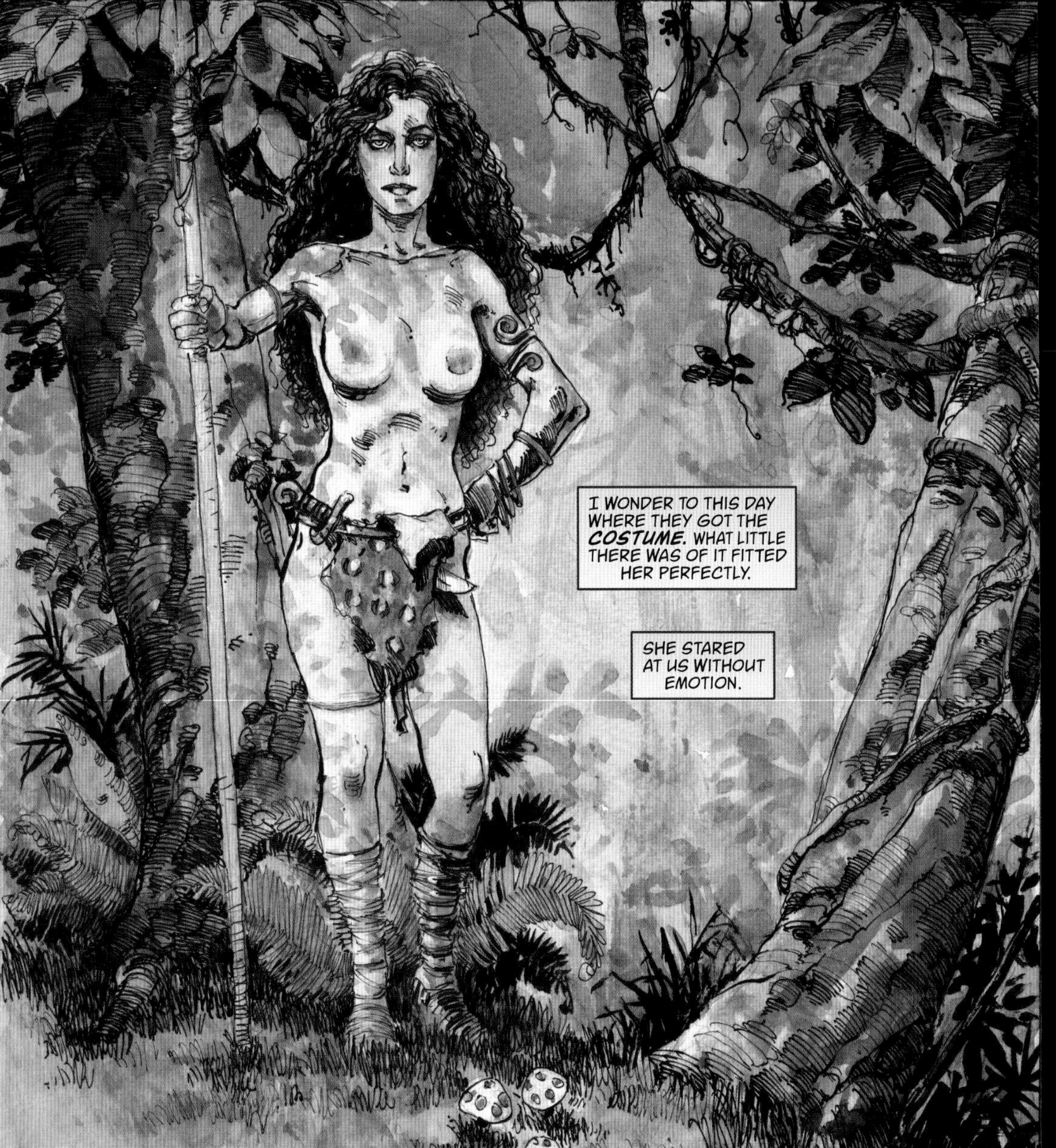
I WONDER TO THIS DAY WHERE THEY GOT THE COSTUME. WHAT LITTLE THERE WAS OF IT FITTED HER PERFECTLY.
SHE STARED AT US WITHOUT EMOTION.

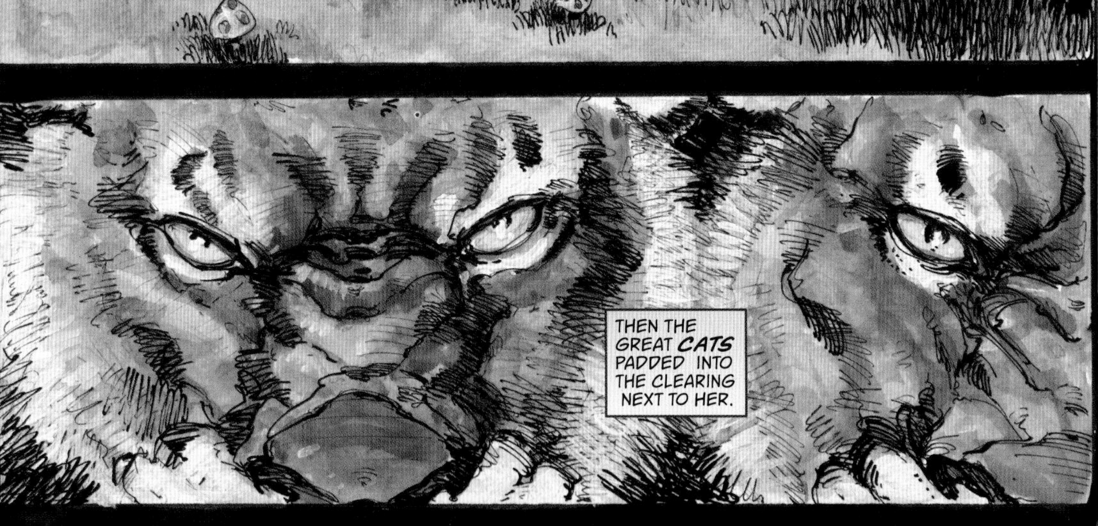
THEN THE GREAT CATS PADDED INTO THE CLEARING NEXT TO HER.

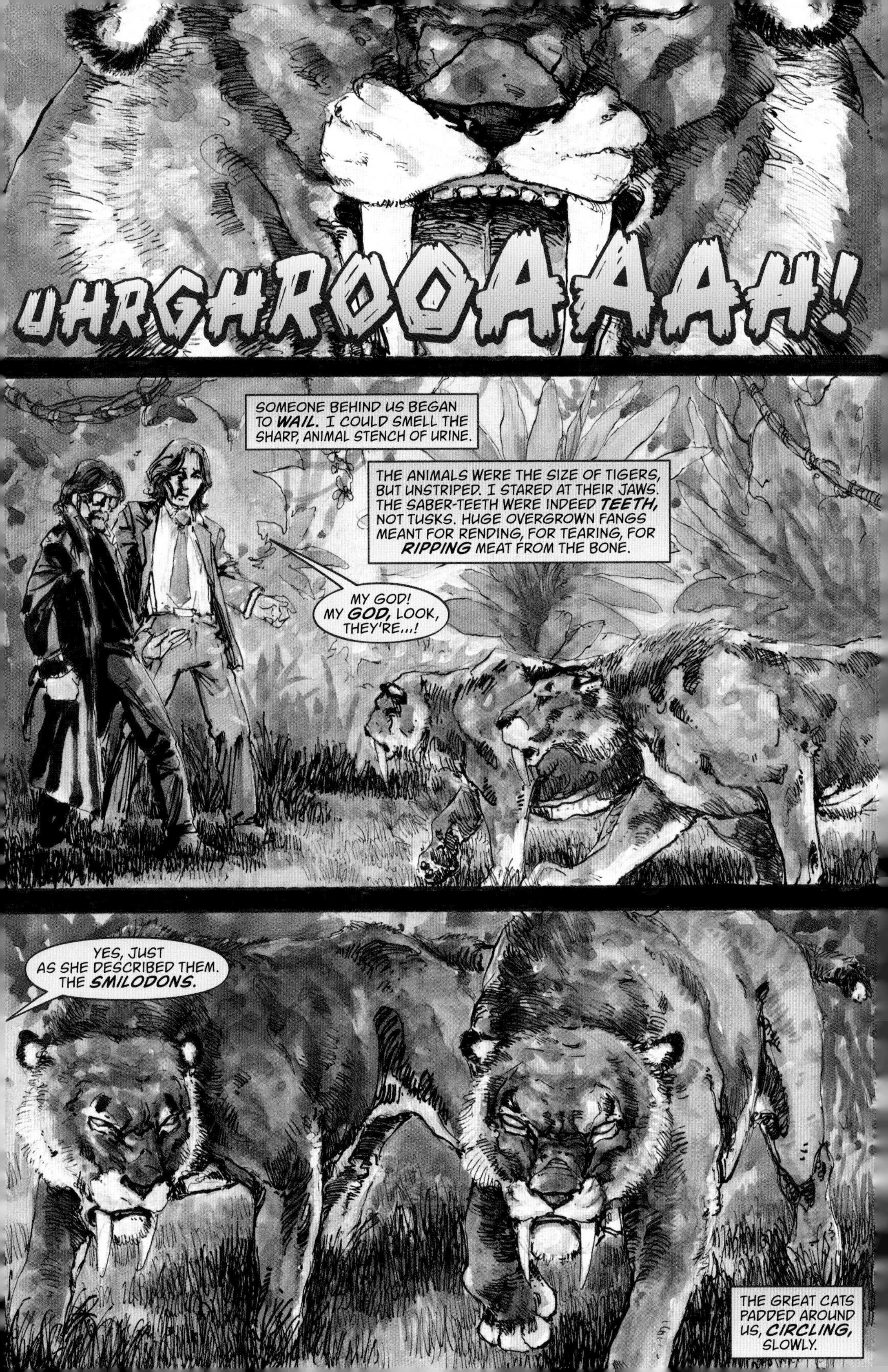
UHRGHROOAAAH!
SOMEONE BEHIND US BEGAN TO WAIL. I COULD SMELL THE SHARP, ANIMAL STENCH OF URINE.
THE ANIMALS WERE THE SIZE OF TIGERS, BUT UNSTRIPED. I STARED AT THEIR JAWS. THE SABER-TEETH WERE INDEED TEETH, NOT TUSKS. HUGE OVERGROWN FANGS MEANT FOR RENDING, FOR TEARING, FOR RIPPING MEAT FROM THE BONE.
MY GOD! MY GOD, LOOK, THEY'RE...!
YES, JUST AS SHE DESCRIBED THEM. THE SMILODONS.
THE GREAT CATS PADDED AROUND US, CIRCLING, SLOWLY.

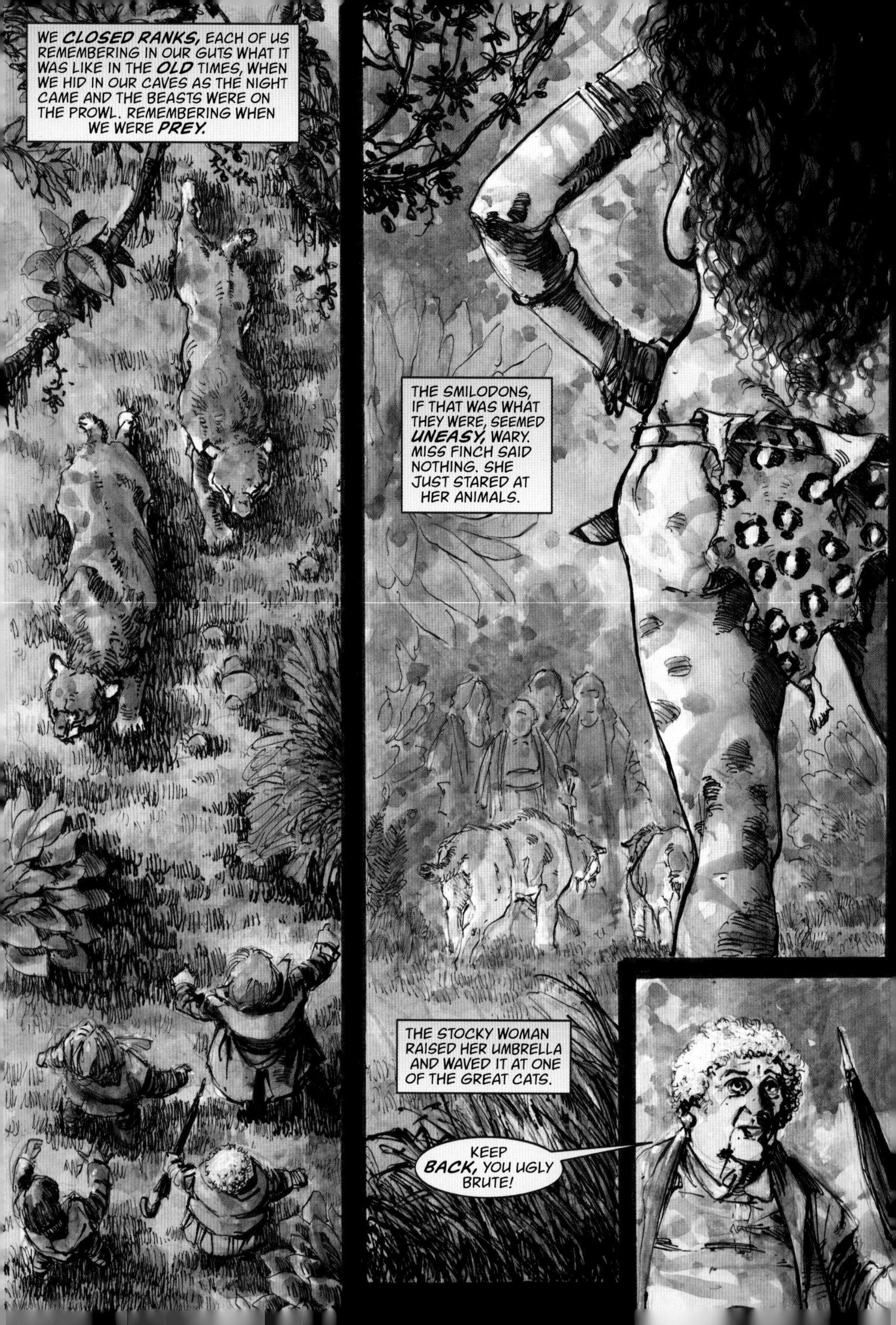
WE CLOSED RANKS, EACH OF US REMEMBERING IN OUR GUTS WHAT IT WAS LIKE IN THE OLD TIMES, WHEN WE HID IN OUR CAVES AS THE NIGHT CAME AND THE BEASTS WERE ON THE PROWL. REMEMBERING WHEN WE WERE PREY.
THE SMILODONS, IF THAT WAS WHAT THEY WERE, SEEMED UNEASY, WARY. MISS FINCH SAID NOTHING. SHE JUST STARED AT HER ANIMALS.
THE STOCKY WOMAN RAISED HER UMBRELLA AND WAVED IT AT ONE OF THE GREAT CATS.
KEEP BACK, YOU UGLY BRUTE!

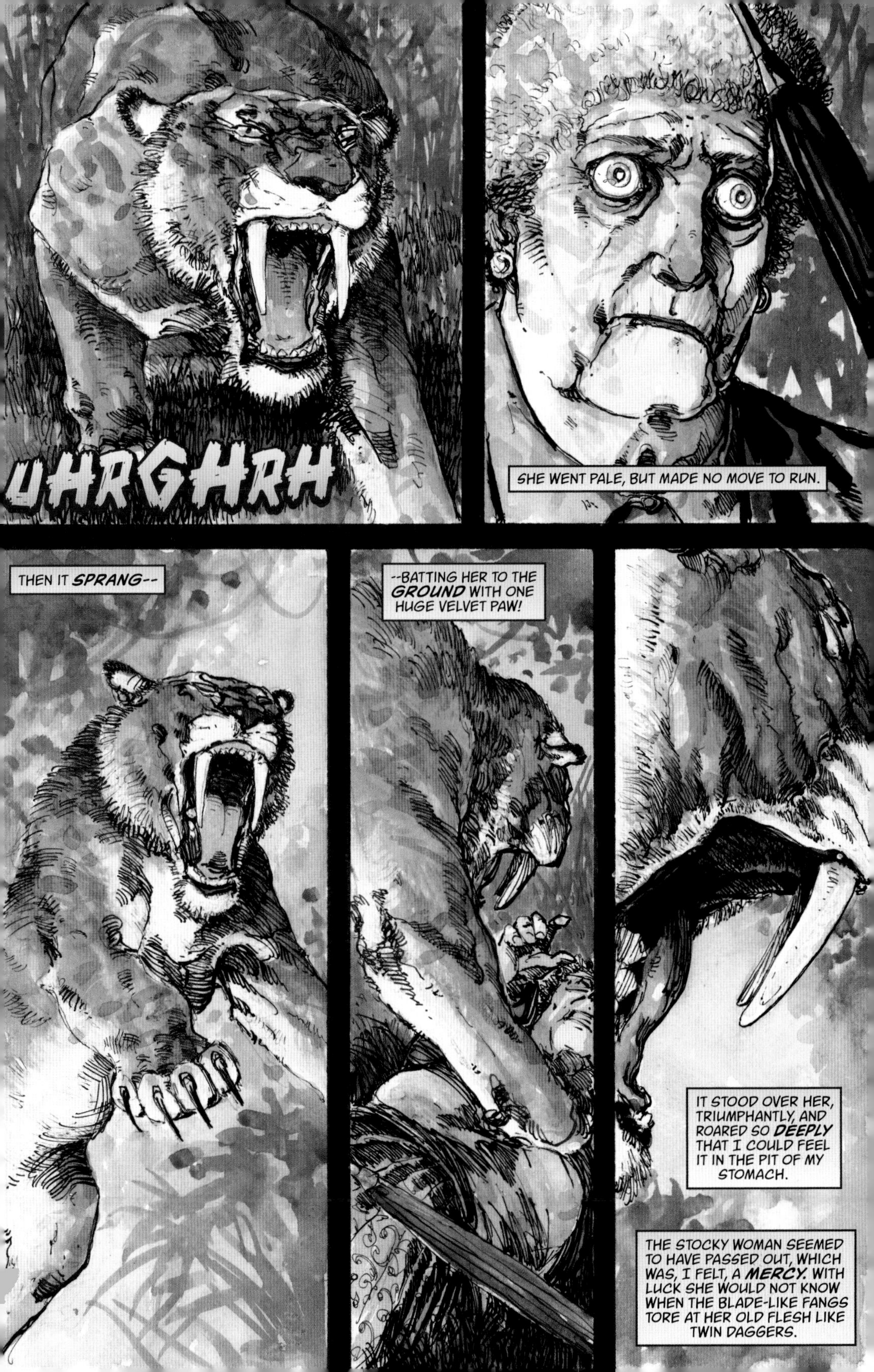
UHRGHRH
SHE WENT PALE, BUT MADE NO MOVE TO RUN.
THEN IT SPRANG--
--BATTING HER TO THE GROUND WITH ONE HUGE VELVET PAW!
IT STOOD OVER HER, TRIUMPHANTLY, AND ROARED SO DEEPLY THAT I COULD FEEL IT IN THE PIT OF MY STOMACH.
THE STOCKY WOMAN SEEMED TO HAVE PASSED OUT, WHICH WAS, I FELT, A MERCY. WITH LUCK SHE WOULD NOT KNOW WHEN THE BLADE-LIKE FANGS TORE AT HER OLD FLESH LIKE TWIN DAGGERS.

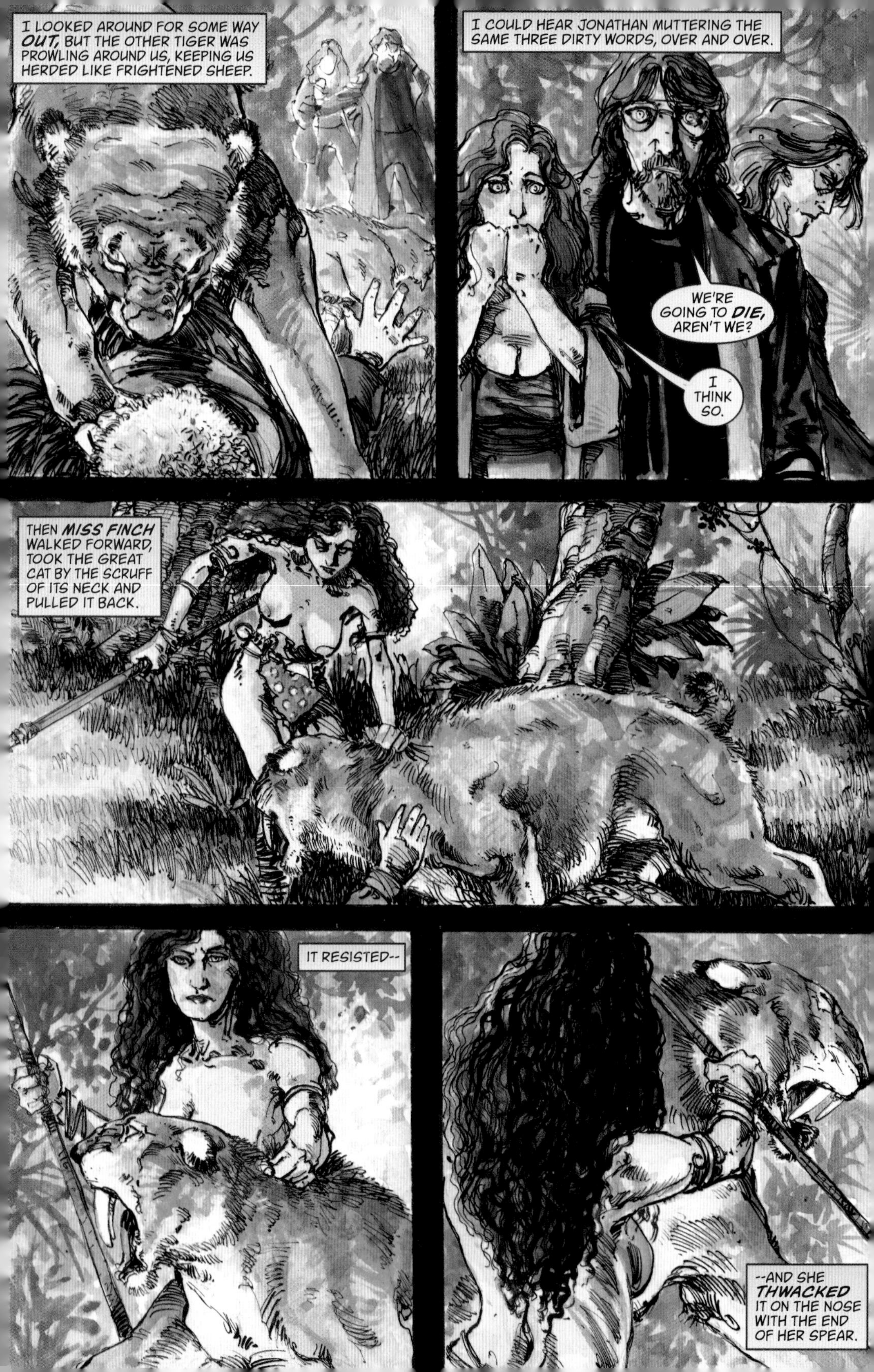
I LOOKED AROUND FOR SOME WAY OUT, BUT THE OTHER TIGER WAS PROWLING AROUND US, KEEPING US HERDED LIKE FRIGHTENED SHEEP.
I COULD HEAR JONATHAN MUTTERING THE SAME THREE DIRTY WORDS, OVER AND OVER.
WE'RE GOING TO DIE, AREN'T WE?
I THINK SO.
THEN MISS FINCH WALKED FORWARD, TOOK THE GREAT CAT BY THE SCRUFF OF ITS NECK AND PULLED IT BACK.
IT RESISTED--
--AND SHE THWACKED IT ON THE NOSE WITH THE END OF HER SPEAR.

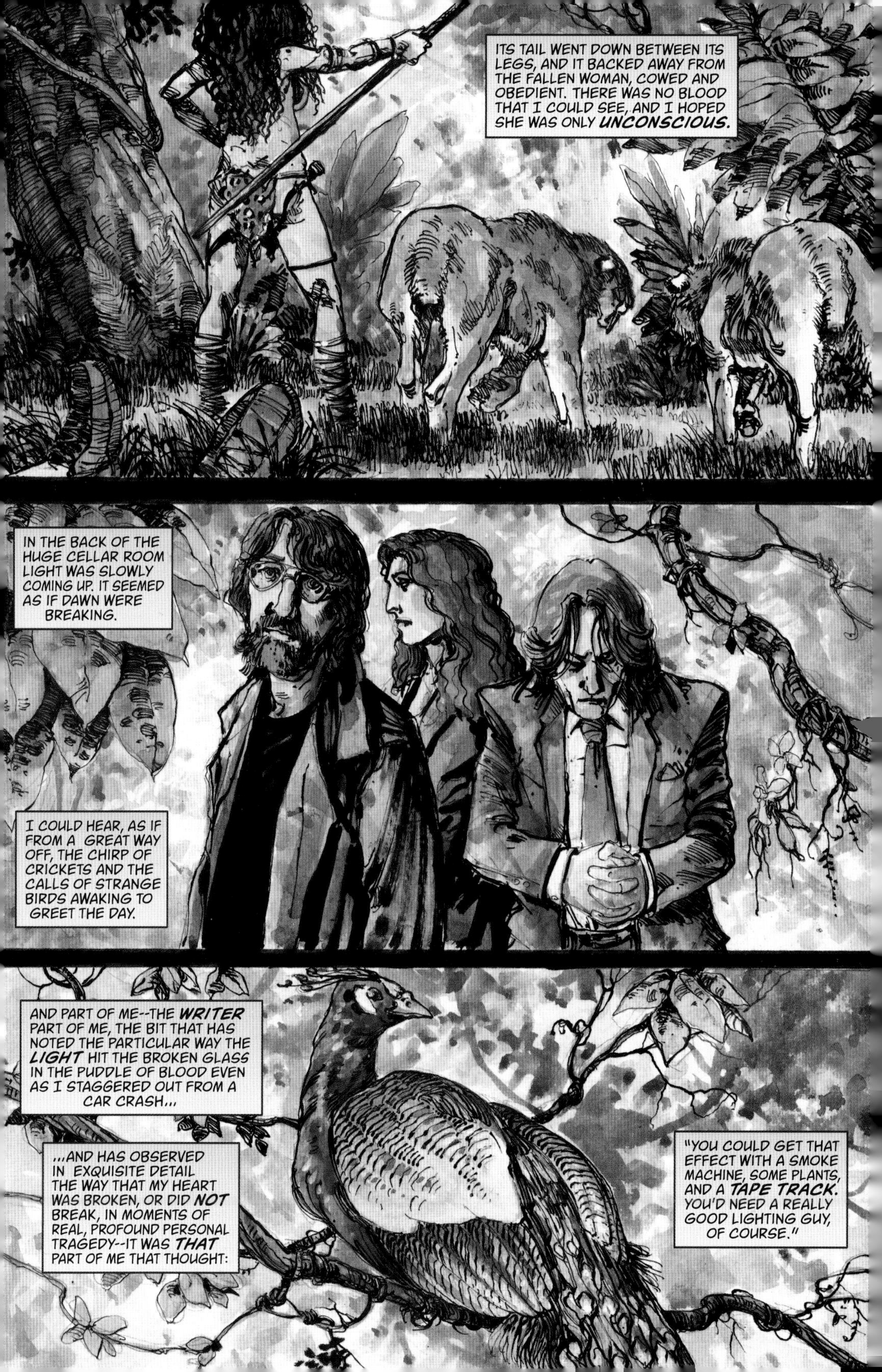
ITS TAIL WENT DOWN BETWEEN ITS LEGS, AND IT BACKED AWAY FROM THE FALLEN WOMAN, COWED AND OBEDIENT. THERE WAS NO BLOOD THAT I COULD SEE, AND I HOPED SHE WAS ONLY UNCONSCIOUS.
IN THE BACK OF THE HUGE CELLAR ROOM LIGHT WAS SLOWLY COMING UP. IT SEEMED AS IF DAWN WERE BREAKING.
I COULD HEAR, AS IF FROM A GREAT WAY OFF, THE CHIRP OF CRICKETS AND THE CALLS OF STRANGE BIRDS AWAKING TO GREET THE DAY.
AND PART OF ME--THE WRITER PART OF ME, THE BIT THAT HAS NOTED THE PARTICULAR WAY THE LIGHT HIT THE BROKEN GLASS IN THE PUDDLE OF BLOOD EVEN AS I STAGGERED OUT FROM A CAR CRASH...
...AND HAS OBSERVED IN EXQUISITE DETAIL THE WAY THAT MY HEART WAS BROKEN, OR DID NOT BREAK, IN MOMENTS OF REAL, PROFOUND PERSONAL TRAGEDY--IT WAS THAT PART OF ME THAT THOUGHT:
"YOU COULD GET THAT EFFECT WITH A SMOKE MACHINE, SOME PLANTS, AND A TAPE TRACK. YOU'D NEED A REALLY GOOD LIGHTING GUY, OF COURSE."

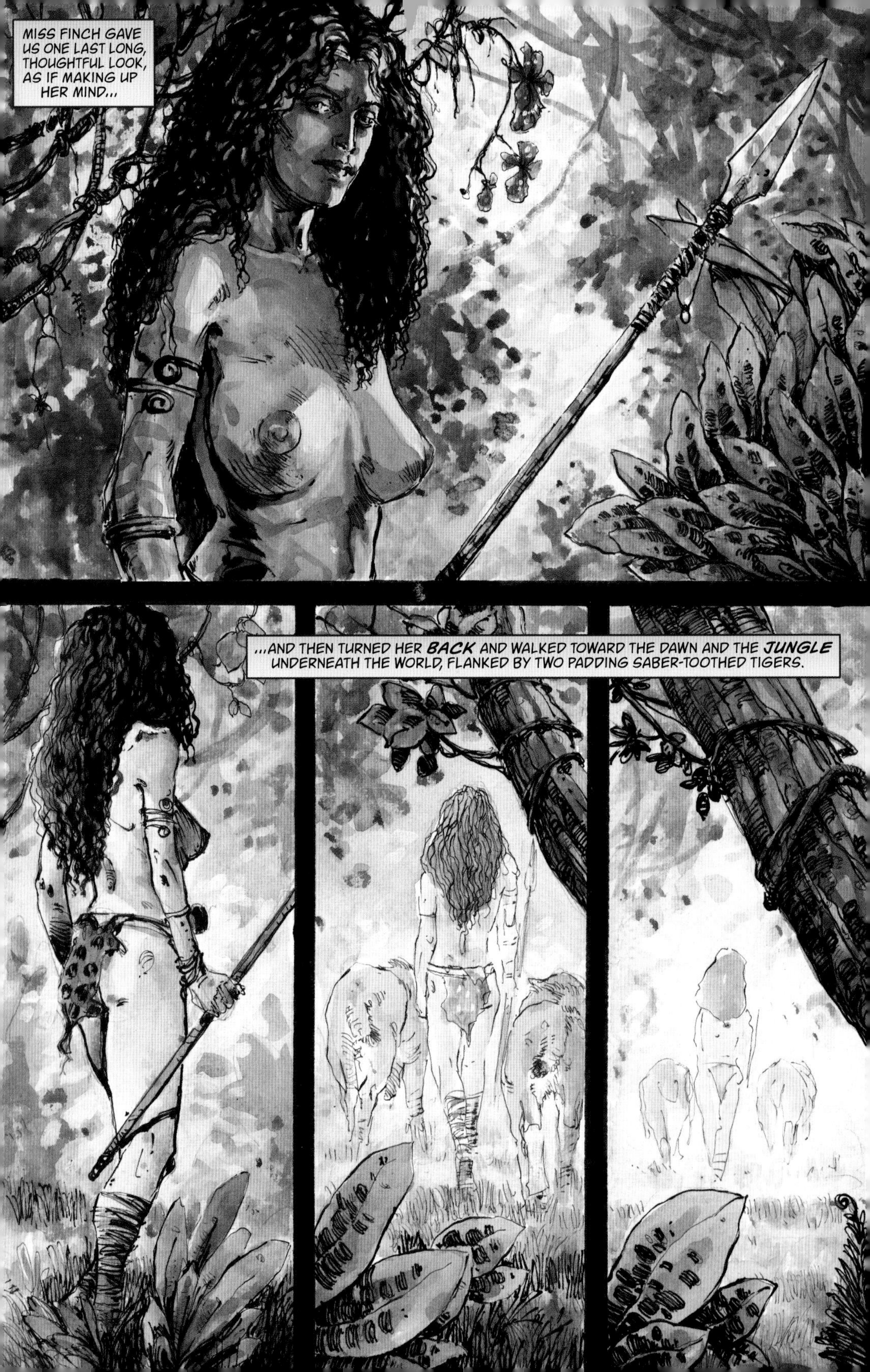
MISS FINCH GAVE US ONE LAST LONG, THOUGHTFUL LOOK, AS IF MAKING UP HER MIND...
...AND THEN TURNED HER BACK AND WALKED TOWARD THE DAWN AND THE JUNGLE UNDERNEATH THE WORLD, FLANKED BY TWO PADDING SABER-TOOTHED TIGERS.

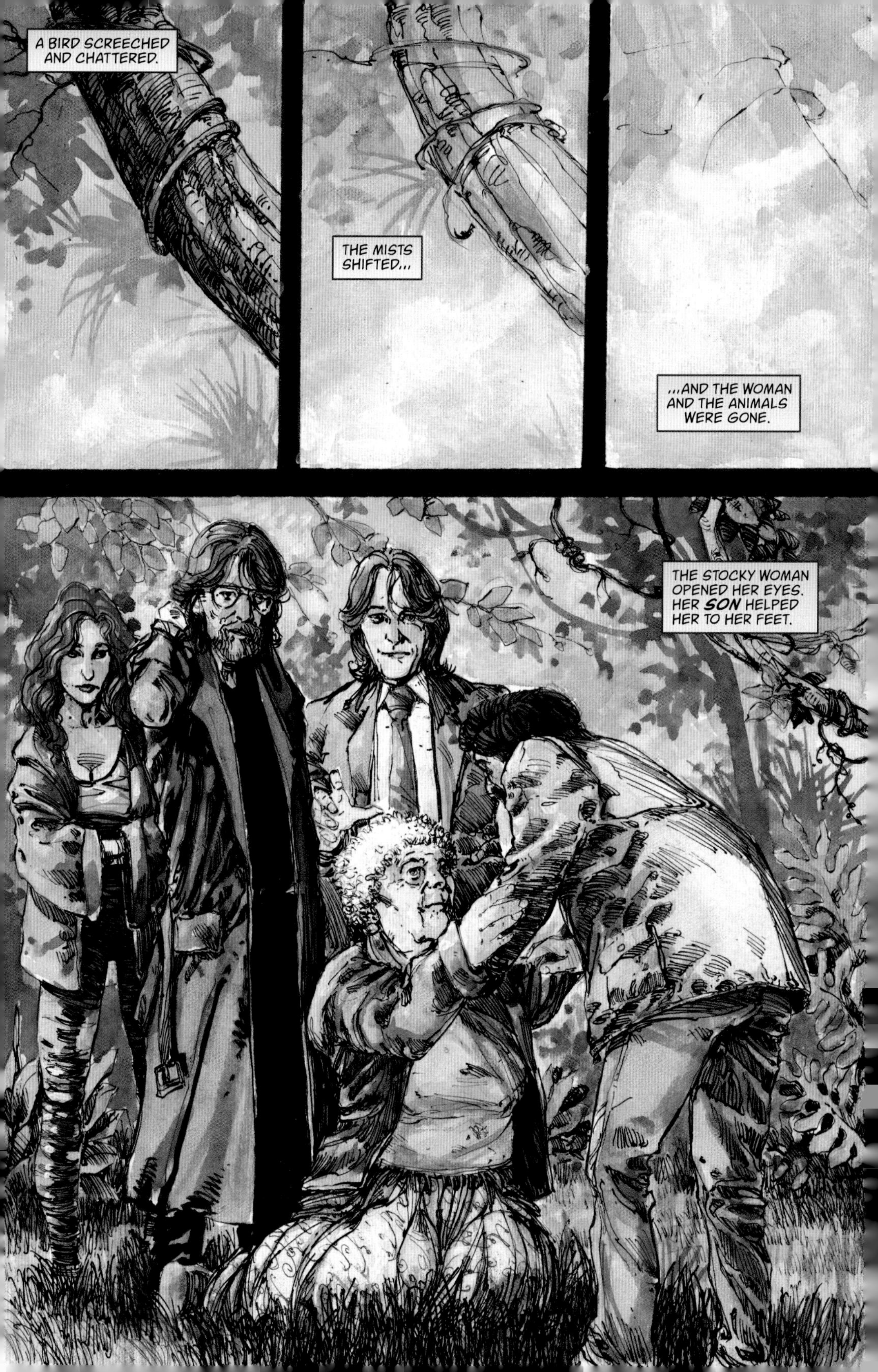
A BIRD SCREECHED AND CHATTERED.
THE MISTS SHIFTED...
...AND THE WOMAN AND THE ANIMALS WERE GONE.
THE STOCKY WOMAN OPENED HER EYES. HER SON HELPED HER TO HER FEET.

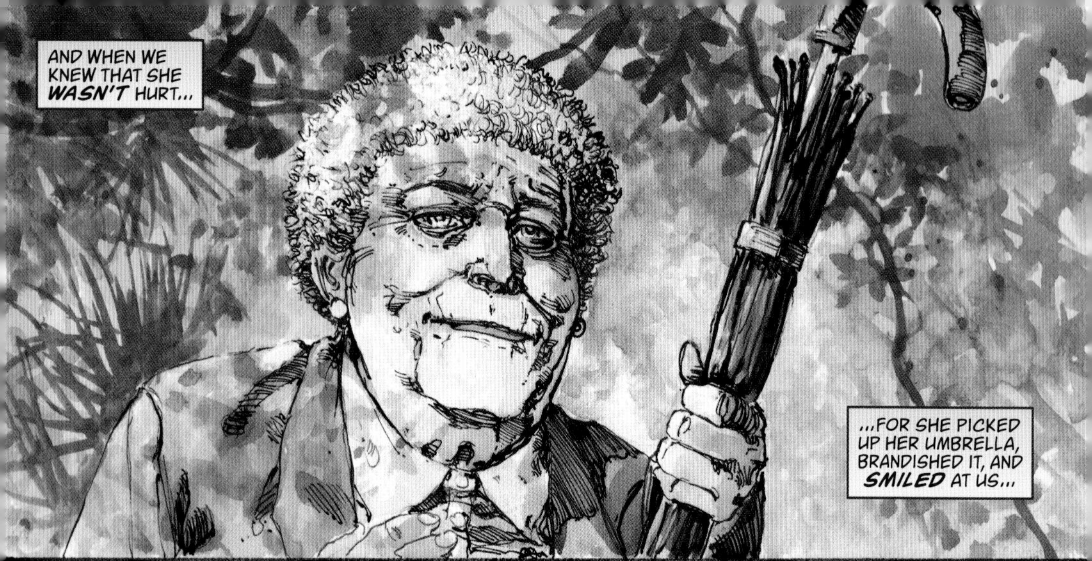
AND WHEN WE KNEW THAT SHE *WASN'T* HURT...
...FOR SHE PICKED UP HER UMBRELLA, BRANDISHED IT, AND *SMILED* AT US...

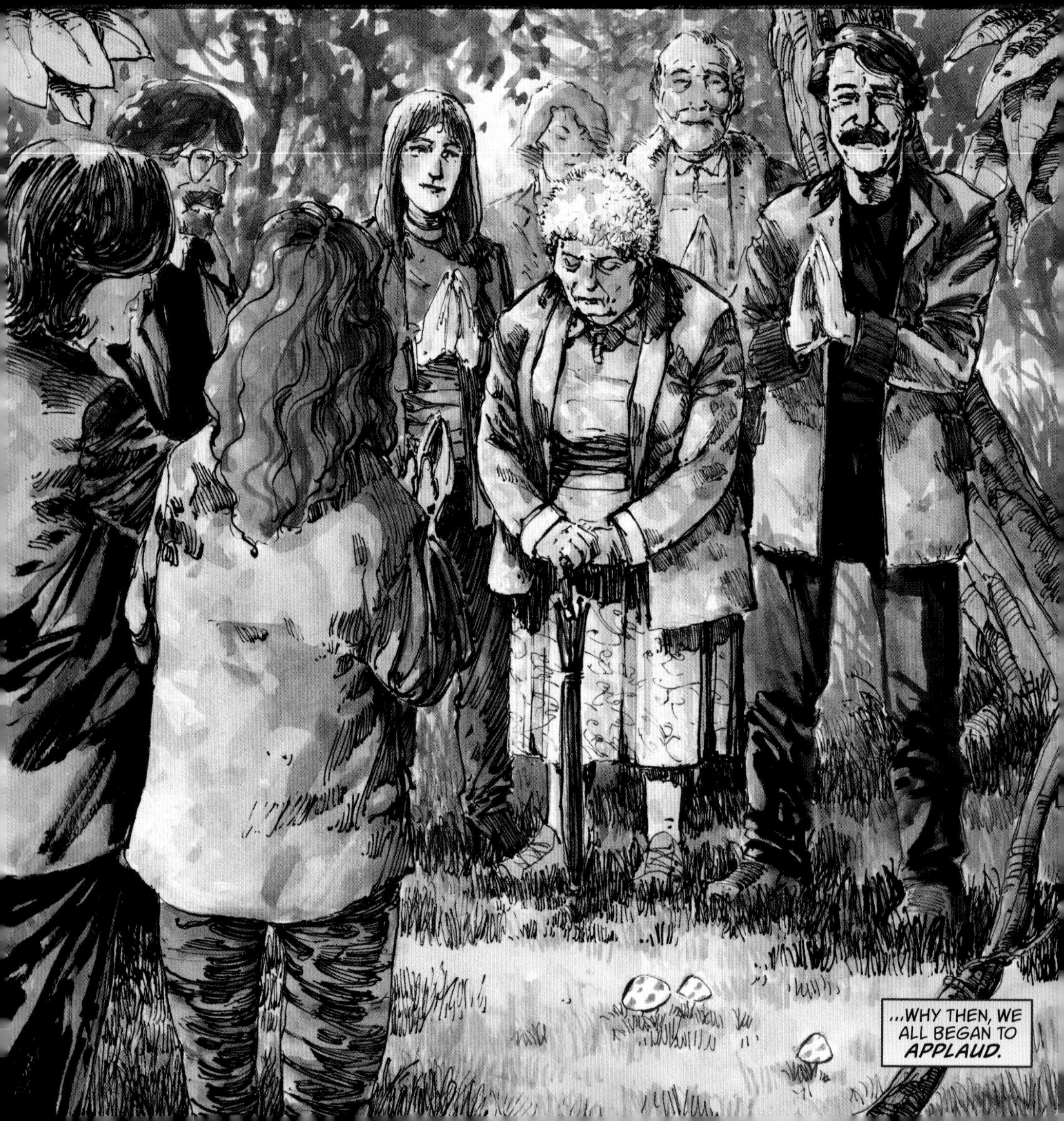
...WHY THEN, WE ALL BEGAN TO *APPLAUD.*

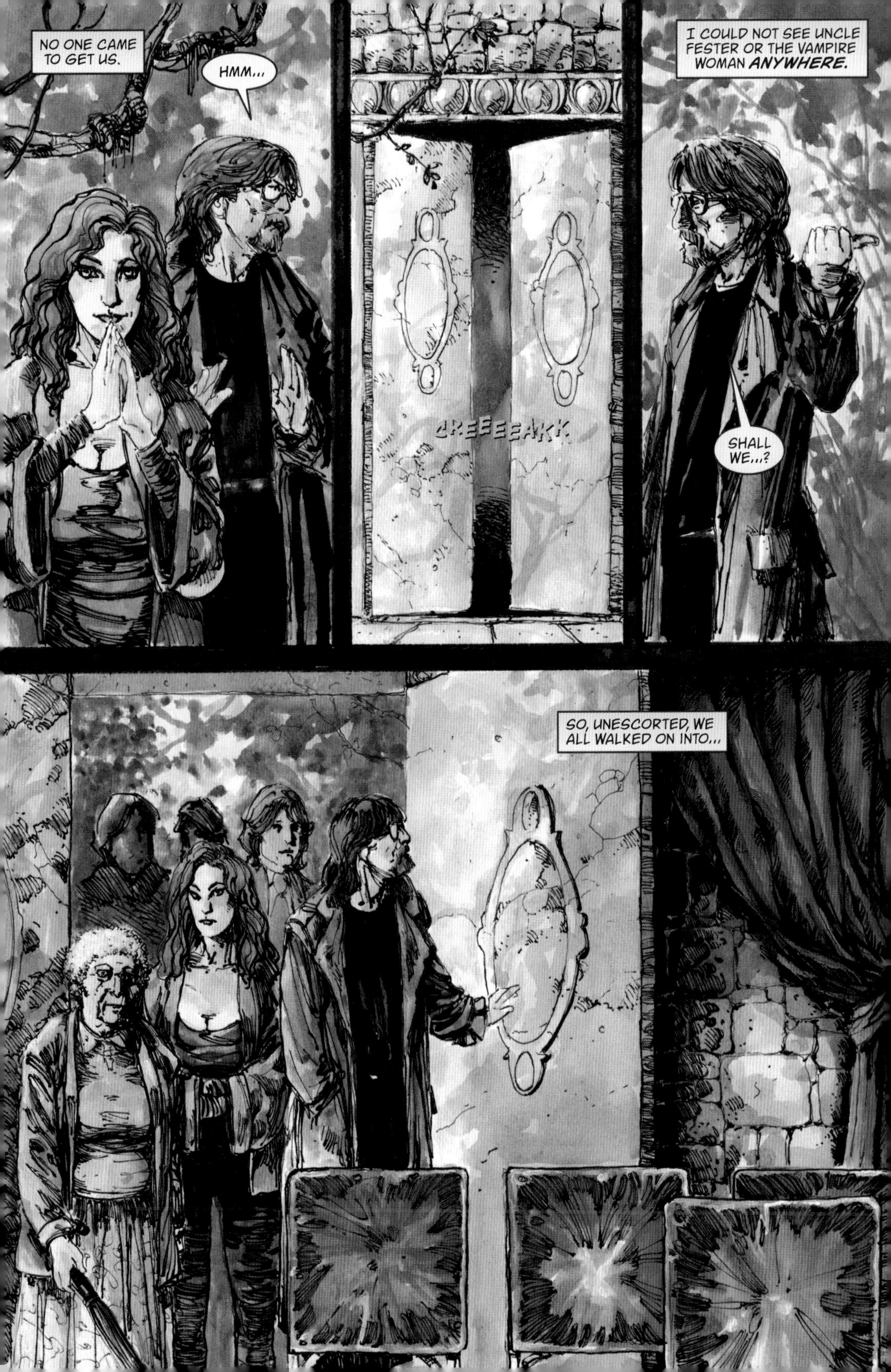
NO ONE CAME TO GET US.
HMM...
CREEEEAKK
I COULD NOT SEE UNCLE FESTER OR THE VAMPIRE WOMAN ANYWHERE.
SHALL WE...?
SO, UNESCORTED, WE ALL WALKED ON INTO...

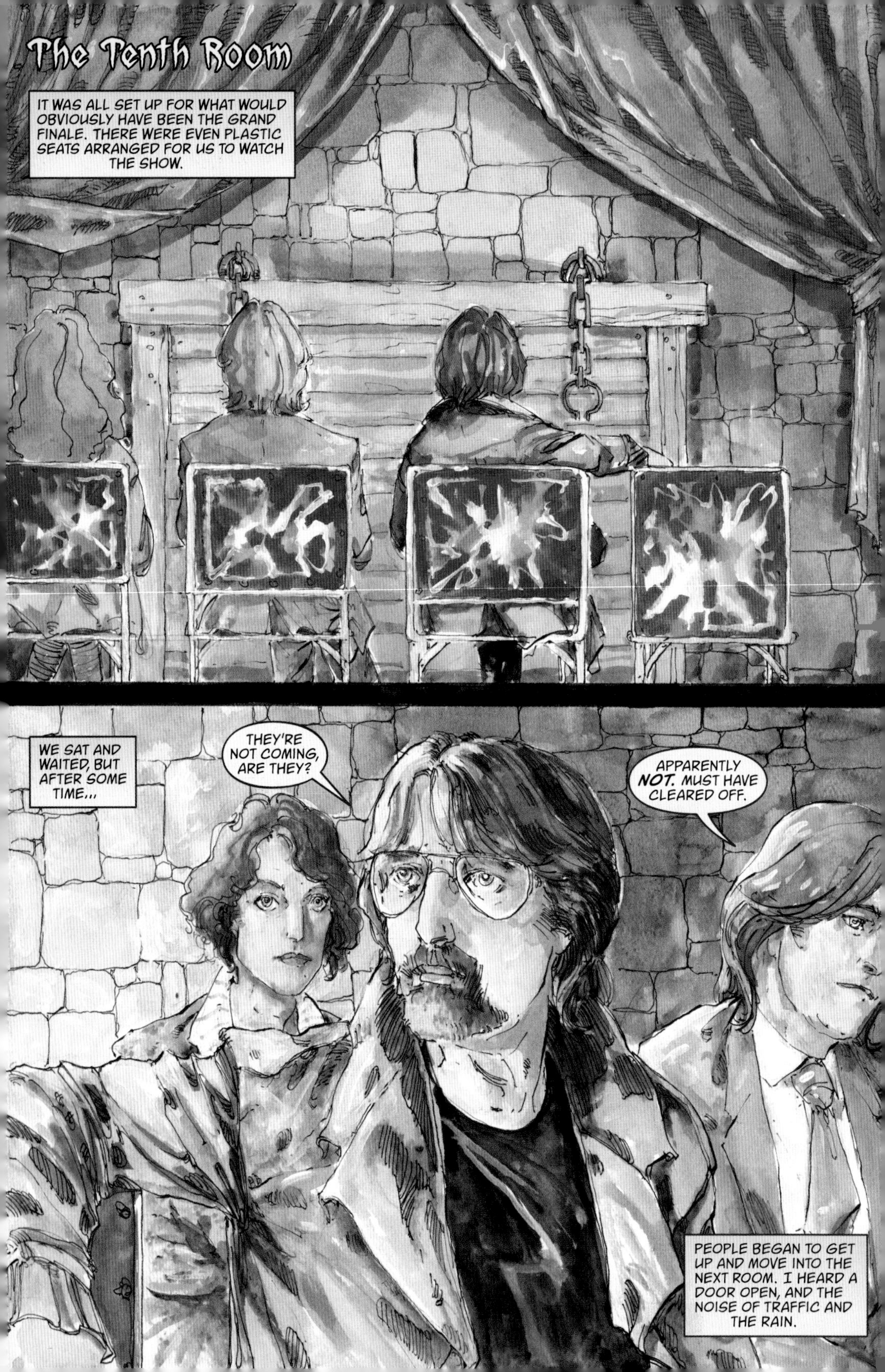
The Tenth Room
IT WAS ALL SET UP FOR WHAT WOULD OBVIOUSLY HAVE BEEN THE GRAND FINALE. THERE WERE EVEN PLASTIC SEATS ARRANGED FOR US TO WATCH THE SHOW.
WE SAT AND WAITED, BUT AFTER SOME TIME...
THEY'RE NOT COMING, ARE THEY?
APPARENTLY NOT. MUST HAVE CLEARED OFF.
PEOPLE BEGAN TO GET UP AND MOVE INTO THE NEXT ROOM. I HEARD A DOOR OPEN, AND THE NOISE OF TRAFFIC AND THE RAIN.

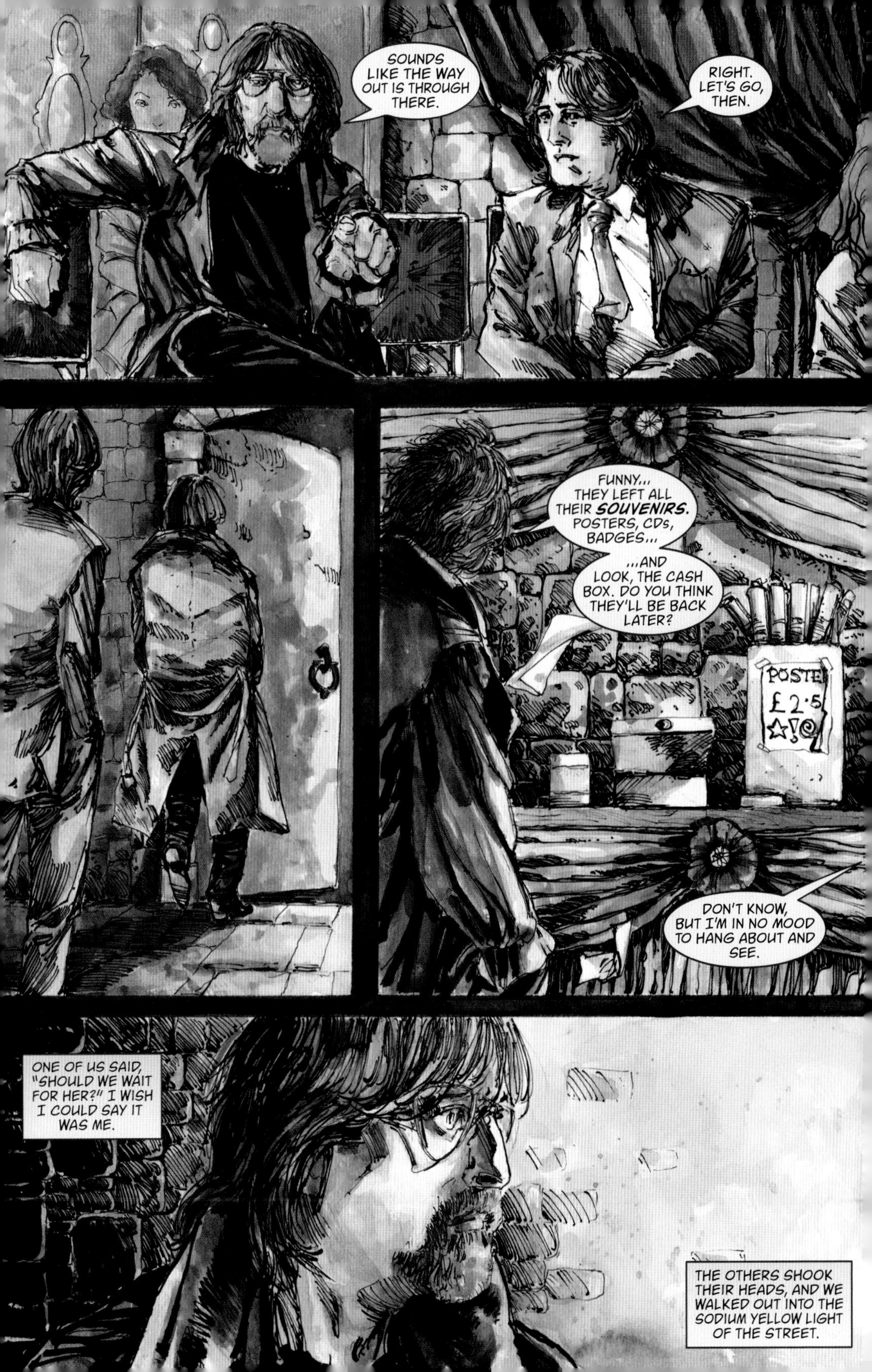
SOUNDS LIKE THE WAY OUT IS THROUGH THERE.
RIGHT. LET'S GO, THEN.
FUNNY... THEY LEFT ALL THEIR SOUVENIRS. POSTERS, CDs, BADGES...
...AND LOOK, THE CASH BOX. DO YOU THINK THEY'LL BE BACK LATER?
POSTE £2.5
DON'T KNOW, BUT I'M IN NO MOOD TO HANG ABOUT AND SEE.
ONE OF US SAID, "SHOULD WE WAIT FOR HER?" I WISH I COULD SAY IT WAS ME.
THE OTHERS SHOOK THEIR HEADS, AND WE WALKED OUT INTO THE SODIUM YELLOW LIGHT OF THE STREET.

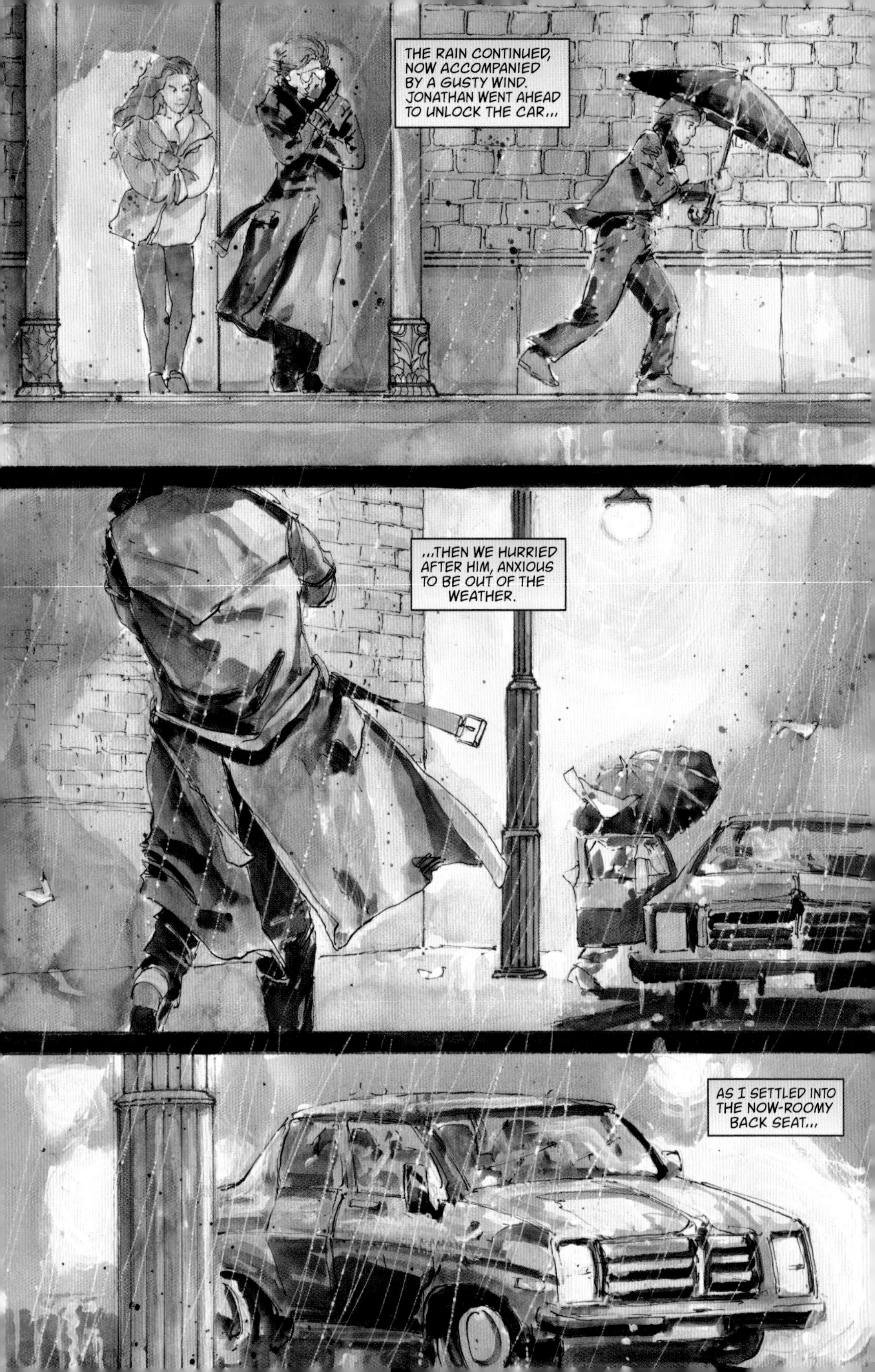
THE RAIN CONTINUED, NOW ACCOMPANIED BY A GUSTY WIND. JONATHAN WENT AHEAD TO UNLOCK THE CAR...
...THEN WE HURRIED AFTER HIM, ANXIOUS TO BE OUT OF THE WEATHER.
AS I SETTLED INTO THE NOW-ROOMY BACK SEAT...

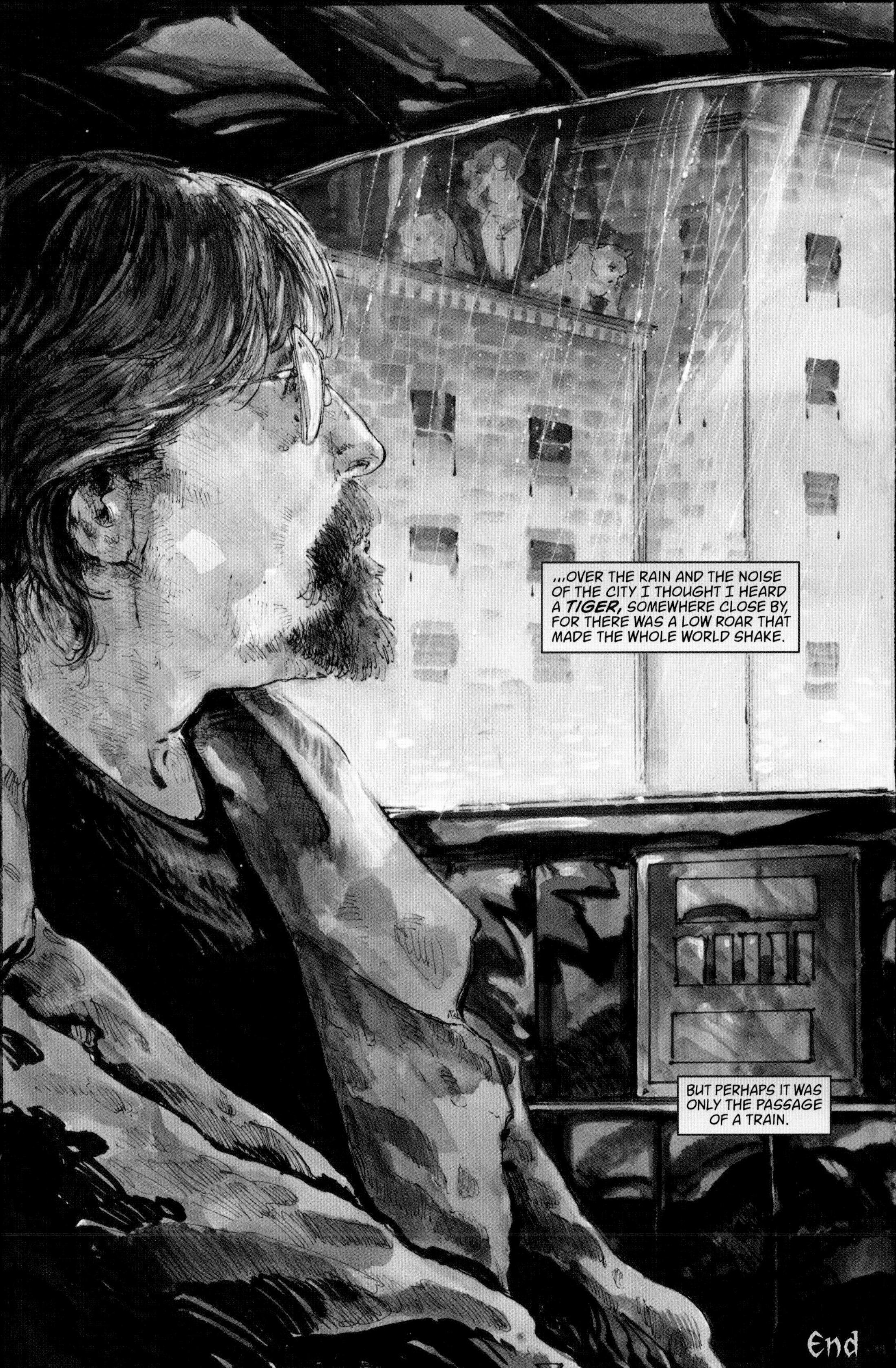
...OVER THE RAIN AND THE NOISE OF THE CITY I THOUGHT I HEARD A **TIGER,** SOMEWHERE CLOSE BY, FOR THERE WAS A LOW ROAR THAT MADE THE WHOLE WORLD SHAKE.
BUT PERHAPS IT WAS ONLY THE PASSAGE OF A TRAIN.
End

❧CREATOR BIOS❧

Photo by Sophia Quach

NEIL GAIMAN is one of the most highly regarded writers of the modern comic book and a prolific creator of prose, poetry, film, journalism, comics, song lyrics, and drama. In 1987, he began his best-known work in comics, the best-selling and award-winning Vertigo series *The Sandman*. Before then, he collaborated with artist Dave McKean on two graphic novels, *Violent Cases* and *Signal to Noise*, both currently available from Dark Horse. Other works with McKean include the comics *Black Orchid* and *The Tragical Comedy or Comical Tragedy of Mr. Punch*, the illustrated children's books *The Day I Swapped My Dad for Two Goldfish* and *The Wolves in the Walls*, and the film *MirrorMask*, which Gaiman wrote and McKean directed. As a novelist, Gaiman has penned three *New York Times* bestsellers: *American Gods*, *Coraline*, and *Anansi Boys*. In 2007, his novel *Stardust* was adapted into a major motion picture, and his script for *Beowulf*, co-written with Roger Avary, was directed by Robert Zemeckis. Collections of his short prose include *Smoke and Mirrors* and *Fragile Things*, and his other comics work includes *The Eternals* and *1602* for Marvel; *The Books of Magic*, *Death: The High Cost of Living*, and *Death: The Time of Your Life* for Vertigo; and *Harlequin Valentine*, *Murder Mysteries*, *The Last Temptation*, and *Creatures of the Night* for Dark Horse. He lives and works near Minneapolis.

Photo by Fhionn

MICHAEL ZULLI began his comics career in 1986 as the artist of *The Puma Blues*, written by Stephen Murphy. Published first by Aardvark-Vanaheim and later by Mirage Studios, the series ran for twenty-three issues and was renowned for its experimental storytelling techniques and message of environmental responsibility. Zulli also plotted, wrote, co-wrote, and illustrated *Soul's Winter*, a Teenage Mutant Ninja Turtles trilogy for Mirage Studios, now available in a collected edition. Going on to illustrate a number of stories in Steve Bissette's horror anthology *Taboo*, Zulli saw his profile skyrocket after becoming one of the artists on Vertigo's best-selling and award-winning series *The Sandman*, written by Neil Gaiman. Frequent artistic collaborators, Zulli and Gaiman have completed several works together in addition to *The Sandman*, including *The Last Temptation*, a dark fable starring rock musician Alice Cooper, and *Creatures of the Night*, featuring two magical tales of humans and animals who are far from what they seem. Zulli was also the illustrator of J. Michael Straczynski's novella *Delicate Creatures*, published by Top Cow Productions. For the past few years he has been writing and illustrating a massive and deeply personal opus, *The Fracture of the Universal Boy*. He currently lives in Minnesota.

Photo by José Villarrubia

TODD KLEIN has established himself as one of the pre-eminent letterers of contemporary comics over the course of his thirty-year career. Beginning in the production department at DC Comics in 1977, he meticulously studied the work of letterers such as John Workman, John Costanza, and Gaspar Saladino, and was soon lettering and designing logos for many titles. During this time, Klein also wrote comics, including stories for *House of Mystery*, *Green Lantern*, and *The Omega Men*. In 1987, he became a full-time freelance letterer, shortly thereafter launching a long-running collaboration with writer Neil Gaiman on *The Sandman* from Vertigo. In addition to Gaiman, Klein has worked with writer Alan Moore for over a decade on numerous projects, including lettering and designing for the America's Best Comics line at Wildstorm. Author of the lettering section in *The DC Comics Guide to Coloring and Lettering Comics*, Klein's mastery has been recognized around the world, most notably with fourteen Eisner Awards and eight Harvey Awards. He continues to work voraciously from his home in New Jersey where he lives with his wife Ellen.

The

NEIL GAIMAN

—LIBRARY—

available in hardcover from Dark Horse Books®

Creatures of the Night
illustrated by Michael Zulli
ISBN 978-1-56971-936-7

Harlequin Valentine
illustrated by John Bolton
ISBN 978-1-56971-620-5

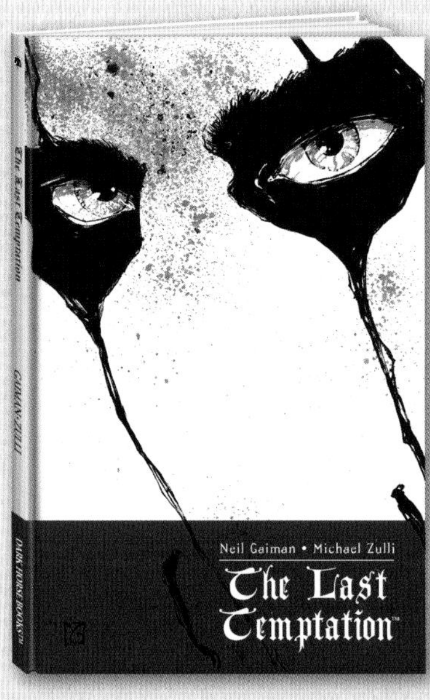

The Last Temptation
illustrated by Michael Zulli
ISBN 978-1-59307-414-2

Murder Mysteries
adapted & illustrated by P. Craig Russell
ISBN 978-1-56971-634-2